The Saga of the Lucky Lou

The Ship the Japs Couldn't Sink

La   'ridley

Copyright © 2012 by Larry Fridley

The Saga of the Lucky Lou
by Larry Fridley

Printed in the United States of America

ISBN 9781624198793

All rights reserved solely by the author. The author guarantees all contents are original and do not infringe upon the legal rights of any other person or work. No part of this book may be reproduced in any form without the permission of the author. The views expressed in this book are not necessarily those of the publisher.

www.xulonpress.com

Acknowledgements

Al Seton

Jack Jones

Michael Backauskas

Ernest Koehler

Douglas Huggins

Nad Peterson

Mary Lou Mohr

Mrs. Harry James for the original typing.

All contributors to this book through their work with the *Hubble Bubble*, the ship's newspaper, which is still in existence today under Editor Jack R. Jones.

Table of Contents

Introduction	xi
Chapter One	13
Chapter Two	18
Chapter Three	27
Chapter Four	42
Chapter Five	51
Chapter Six	64
Chapter Seven	72
Chapter Eight	81
Chapter Nine	101
Chapter Ten	115
Chapter Eleven	129
Chapter Twelve	146
Chapter Thirteen	153
Chapter Fourteen	184
Chapter Fifteen	199
Conclusion	211
Selected Bibliography	239

"Oh! Give me land, lots of land, under U.S. skies above.

Don't ship me out.

Let me ride on those over-crowded street cars that I love.

Don't ship me out.

Let me be by myself in the warm spring rain and listen to the rumble of the subway train.

Keep me here forever and I won't complain!

Don't ship me out.

Just turn me loose, let me straddle my old saddle under neon signs above.

In my dress blues, let me gander and meander, till I see that one I love.

I want to ride to the city where the fun commences,

and gaze at the women till I lose all my senses.

Can't take to water, but I don't mind fences…

Don't ship me out!"

–Larry Fridley

U.S.S. Helena - Sister Ship to U.S.S. St. Louis

Introduction

The cruiser USS *St. Louis* (CL 49) had its origin on February 13, 1929, when Congress authorized fifteen new cruisers for the totally cruiser-deficient U.S. Navy. Five years later, on March 27, 1934, Congress appropriated the money for these cruisers.

As the Navy began to build these new cruisers, it also began changing its fleet training programs to meet the kind of conditions which ships would face in a future war. Although warned repeatedly that the Japanese Navy was specializing in night fighting, very little such training was adopted by the U.S. Navy; nor did the United States make improvements in its poorly designed- and more poorly performing- torpedoes. On the other hand, the U.S. Navy planners made great strides in developing centrally directed gunfire. The *St. Louis* was an outstanding example of these advancements.

Before the keels for these new cruisers had even been laid, the Japanese had developed—about 1933—and perfected a torpedo vastly superior in every aspect of performance to ours. Equally remarkable is that although the Japanese used their new torpedo—the Model 93, or "Long Lance"—for eight pre-war years, its capabilities were unknown to the United States. This half-ton monster packed twice the explosive charge of the American torpedo, and could travel 11 miles at 49 knots while ours could only travel 7.5 miles at 26.5 knots. In fact, at 36 knots the oxygen-fueled Long Lance torpedo could travel twice as far—outreaching even the guns of a battleship. Each Japanese destroyer carried eight torpedo tubes which could be reloaded in a remarkably fast time of eighteen minutes. While we removed torpedo tubes from our old cruisers and manufactured new cruisers without them, the Japanese continued to arm their cruisers with torpedoes.

The *St. Louis*, named in honor of the city of St. Louis, Missouri, was the fourth naval vessel to carry this name; it was fifteen times as large as the first sloop-of-war *St. Louis*, built a century earlier. The keel was laid in Newport News, Virginia, December 10, 1936; it was christened and launched April 15, 1938.

Chapter One

All was quiet but for the rhythmic hammering of the workmen below at Shipway Six on Friday, April 15, 1938. A crowd had gathered to witness the christening and launch of USS *St. Louis*.

Spring hats and parasols vied with the bunting which decorated the ship and the grandstand. Tugs and small craft drifted lazily at a respectful distance in the Maes River. The hammering stopped—quiet—at the sound of the warning whistle. Cmdr. Herbert Dumstrey, Navy chaplain at the Norfolk Naval Base, offered this prayer:

"Eternal God, Creator of the Universe and Governor of Nations, we have met here to launch this vessel into the service of a nation founded upon the principles of the freedom of religion and the brotherhood of man. Most heartily we beseech Thee with Thy favor to behold and bless Thy servant the President of these United States and all of the officers of our government, and so replenish them with Thy spirit, that they may always incline to Thy will and walk in Thy ways.

We dedicate this vessel not to the service of war, but rather in the interests of peace: "When a strong man armed keepeth his palace, his goods are in peace." We pray that on duty assigned, this vessel shall never turn back, but ever shall sweep to the swift completion of her allotted task. In victory, may mercy temper triumph and in extremity, may no friend or foe ever look in vain to her for succor.

Graciously bless the officers and men of our Navy. May love of country be engraven on their hearts and may their severe toils be duly appreciated by a grateful nation. Behind the day's duty, may they ever see the mighty outline of the Republic itself, which has stood for the glory of God and the peace of the world. If ever our ships of war should be engaged in battle, grant that their struggles may only be under an enforced necessity for the defense of what is right.

Hasten the time when the principles of holy religion shall so prevail upon all nations that none shall wage war for the purpose of aggression and none shall need it as a means of defense.

These blessings we ask through the merits of our Redeemer."

Miss Nancy Lee Morrill, who had been named the "Veiled Prophet Queen of St. Louis" in 1937, was coached by the president of the ship-building company, Howard L. Ferguson, while she swung a bottle of champagne against the prow of the craft as it started toward the water.

Nancy Lee Morrill

Chapter One

"The Birth of a Soul"

Down the ways with a hearty roar,
    down to an eager sea,
In swelling pride the salty tide,
    enveloped her tenderly.
And a lonely gull as he glided by,
    returned from an ocean trip,
Blinked his eyes in great surprise
    at the sight of the mighty ship.
"Down there lies my future home,
    a name for herself she'll earn.
'Till the day I die, I'll proudly fly over
    the wake that she casts astern."
Down in the depths of the slimy deep,
    down where the phantoms lurk,
A black squid peered and harshly jeered
    and his tentacles writhed in the murk.
"This Ship of Ships, this Queen of Queens,
    does not seem so to me.
If she'll float, she'll sink, I'm apt to think,
    and then where will you be?
A maze of steel, inanimate thing
    that has no heart or soul,
I cannot see how destiny,
    has given her a role."
Down from the sky with a gentle swoop,
    down from a cloudy ceiling,
The sea gull heard his every word,
    and said to the squid with feeling,
"How wrong you are, you sulky fish,
    you evil pessimist.
I swear by the stars and the planet Mars,
    a spirit does exist.
It dwells in the hearts of the fearless men
    that sail her across the sea.
I do not feint, this ship is a 'Saint',
    with a noble destiny."

        By C.P. Reed, FC3c, USN

The Saga of the Lucky Lou

Orders of the Day

Monday 7 August	1430 Rehearse "Cast" recovery method 1600 Collision drill followed by abandon ship.
Tuesday 8 August	0930 Captain's inspection. 1300 All deck divisions hold school instructing in deck seamanship and gunnery drills. Air operations ("Baker" or "Cast" recoveries.)
Wednesday 9 August	0915-1015 Instruction for engineer divisions for men of the section having had the 0400-0800 watch. 0915-1130 Gunnery drills followed by air operations. 1015-1100 Engineering casualty drills. 1300-1430 "E" division instruction in paralleling ship's service generators. 1300-1430 Gunnery drills.
Thursday 10 August	0915-1130 "General Quarters," followed by engineering and gunnery instructions, and air operations and engineering casualty drills. 1300-1500 Emergency Drills: a) Fire drill. b) Plane crash drill. c) Fire and rescue drill. d) Steering casualty drill.
Friday 11 August	0815 Hold general field day. Dry down by 1000. Make all preparations for entering port. 1300 Enter Kingston harbor and anchor.
Saturday 12 August	Port routine omitting inspection.
Sunday 13 August	Holiday routine.

D. A. Spencer
Commander, USN
Executive Officer

Chapter One

1939

Leave Kingston	Tues. 15 Aug.
Arrive Port of Spain, Trinidad	Fri. 18 Aug.
Leave Port of Spain	Tues. 22 Aug.
Arrive Ponta Delgada, Azores	Tues. 29 Aug.
Leave Ponta Delgada	Tues. 5 Sept.
Arrive Funchal, Medeira	Thurs. 7 Sept.
Leave Funchal	Mon. 11 Sept.
Arrive Newport, Rhode Island	Mon. 18 Sept.
Leave Newport	Wed. 20 Sept.
Arrive New York City	Thurs. 21 Sept.
Leave New York City	Thurs. 28 Sept.
Arrive Hampton Roads	Fri. 29 Sept.

Total Distance Traveled 8500
Days at Sea 25
Days in Port 28
Total Cruise Days 53

Captain C. H. Morrison, USN Commanding Officer

Commander D. A. Spencer, USN Executive Officer

Chapter Two

On August 29, 1939, the *St. Louis,* then one of the newest ships in the world, arrived in Ponta Del Gada in the Azores on its shakedown cruise. Thus, its position at the outbreak of World War II was 2,300 miles east of New York City and 780 miles from Lisbon, the nearest European port.

On September 1, 1939, Hitler invaded Poland. Two days later, France and Great Britain declared war on Germany. Europe plunged into World War II.

The Navy told the *St. Louis* to stay put, and to leave the Azores in thirty days for a speed run along the coast of Africa.

The German navy had a modest submarine fleet of fifty-six U-boats when World War II began. Only forty-three were ready for combat. Twenty-five of these were 250-ton coastal submarines. The others were 500 or 750-ton, and proved to be the most effective. Hitler and most of his advisors were air-minded and counted on rapid conquest of Europe rather than a protracted war of attrition at sea.

The British, in the twenty years preceding World War II, expended their limited funds on large warships and now faced a shortage of escort vehicles for convoy duty. At first, Hitler opposed increasing the submarine force, but by the end of 1941 their numbers had increased noticeably.

On September 3, a small 650-ton coastal U-boat sank the British liner S.S. Athenia off Ireland to begin the bloody Battle of the Atlantic. In the next few months, almost seventy allied ships would be sunk, at a small cost to the Germans of twenty of their original seagoing U-boats. By the end of World War II in Europe, the

Chapter Two

Germans would claim the sinking of 2700 allied and neutral ships, with a German loss of 783 U-boats and 32,000 German sailors.

On September 5, 1939, President Roosevelt issued a Proclamation of Neutrality, placing an immediate embargo on shipping arms and munitions to all belligerents.

On September 8, President Roosevelt proclaimed a limited national emergency, raising naval manpower ceilings and authorizing the recall to active duty of personnel on the retired and reserved lists. The total active duty strength of the U.S. Naval Service on June 30, 1939, was 125,202 Navy and 19,432 Marines; by June 30, 1940 this strength had increased only to 160,997 Navy and 28,345 Marines. The influence which this war would have on the United States was still uncertain.

On September 14, the Navy ordered 40 of the 110 decommissioned World War I destroyers, which were tied up in rivers and harbors, back into commission. At this time, the U.S. Navy had only 30 destroyers in the Atlantic Squadron—there was no fleet in the Atlantic then—most of which were old 4-stack destroyers. The U.S. Navy began to patrol offshore from the Guiana's to Newfoundland. A short time later, naval aviation and Coast Guard units joined in the surveillance. The U.S. Navy had not been prepared for anti-submarine warfare. This was also the case with the British navy.

Also taking a heavy toll on British shipping were the German surface raiders prowling the Atlantic. One of these was the battleship "Graf Spee," which sank at least nine ships before she was scuttled off to Montevideo, Uraguay on December 17, 1939.

On October 2, 1939, Congress established a neutral zone around the Americas, with the exception of Canada. The U.S. Navy was assigned the mission of maintaining this patrol. It was then that the *St. Louis* was assigned to neutrality patrol, and ordered back to the Americas. The next order of business was to make the run from Norfolk to South America, to Bermuda, and back to Norfolk.

On October 9, 1939, President Roosevelt wrote—in part—to the acting Secretary of the Navy, Charles Edison:

> 2) When any aircraft or surface ship sights a submarine, a report thereof will be rushed to the Navy Department for immediate

action. The plane or surface ship sighting a submarine will remain in contact as long as possible.
3) Planes or Navy or Coast Guard ships may report the sighting of any submarine or suspicious surface ship in plain English to Force Commander or Department.

Thus, the *St. Louis* and a handful of ships and men, a mixture of the oldest and newest of warships all below complement, began and continued for two years the "Neutrality Patrol" of World War II.

Then on November 4, 1939, at the request of the President, Congress repealed the arms embargo and authorized for "cash-and-carry" export of arms and munitions to belligerent powers. At the same time, President Roosevelt asked for a "moral embargo" against Japan because of the bombing of open cities in China during their war there.

In the first stage, the aim of the neutrality patrol was simply the observation and reporting of belligerent vessels. The task which was now laid out for the U.S. Navy was enormous. It was a task too great for one country.

New Year's Day 1940, like Christmas the week before, found the *St. Louis* at sea on neutrality patrol.

"Not one of us would select being at sea on both Christmas and New Year's as our 'first choice' way to observe this happy time of the year," Capt. C. H. Morrison, the first commanding officer of the St. Louis, told the ship's company.

"If we could live our lives on 'first choices' or even 'second choices', what a different place this world would be for us," he continued. "Actually, things just do not work out that way and we find ourselves continuously adjusting our lives to those circumstances which we cannot control, and endeavoring to be sensible enough to come up smiling no matter what happens."

A somewhat antiquated U.S. Navy, which spanned one ocean but was attempting a two-ocean task, was making full use of its newest warship; a ship which, in a few years, would become the last of the world's true gunships.

Following the conquest of Poland by Hitler and Russia, the war in Europe seemed more like a "phony" war than a real one. Public

Chapter Two

opinion in the United States was greatly divided on what the policy should be. The Great Debate in the United States was between the isolationists and the interventionists.

On January 3, 1940, President Roosevelt requested $1.8 billion for national defense and a new appropriation of $1.182 billion. At that time, the U.S. Army compared in size to that of Belgium's army. The U.S. Air Force had about 160 modern fighters and some 50 modern heavy bombers—or about enough planes to participate for a day or two in the air battles which were about to begin over the English Channel.

On April 9, the Nazis invaded Denmark and Norway. On May 10, they invaded Netherlands, Belgium and Luxembourg. At the same time, Winston Churchill stepped into his role as Prime Minister of Great Britain. On May 12, the Nazis invaded France. By May 14, it was apparent France would fall.

Late that night, Churchill met with American Ambassador Joseph Kennedy. When the Ambassador left Churchill at about 1:00 a.m., he sent a special cable in code to President Roosevelt reviewing the situation in Europe, and adding that Churchill said "it was his intention to ask for the loan of thirty or forty of our old destroyers and also whatever airplanes we could spare right now."

On May 15, Churchill cabled President Roosevelt, reporting "the scene has darkened swiftly... The small countries are simply smashed up, one by one, like matchwood... We expect to be attacked here ourselves, both from the air and by parachute and airborne troops in the near future... All I ask now is that you should proclaim non-belligerency, which would mean that you would help us with everything short of actually engaging armed forces. Immediate needs are, first of all, the loan of forty or fifty of your older destroyers to bridge the gap between what we have now and the large new construction we put in hand at the beginning of the war. This time next year we shall have plenty. But if in the interval Italy comes in against us with another hundred submarines we may be strained to the breaking point..."

On May 16, President Roosevelt sent a message to Congress asking for production of 50,000 planes a year. This "unbelievable goal" led Hitler to say "Roosevelt is a sick brain." From early 1940 to the end of World War II, the United States actually produced 296,601 planes—an average of almost 60,000 a year.

President Roosevelt replied to Churchill: "First. With regard to the possible loan of forty or fifty of our older destroyers. As you know, a step of that kind could not be taken except with specific authorization of the Congress and I am not certain that it would be wise for that suggestion to be made to Congress at this moment..."

On June 22, 1940, France fell. Hitler looked forward to a speedy end of the war with Britain, but began crafting plans for an invasion if it should become necessary. The Nazis then launched an air assault on England, which came to be called the Battle of Britain. With the fall of France, and the Mediterranean route closed to British merchant shipping, thousands of miles were added to convoys going to and from England.

On June 26, King George VI wrote a personal letter to Roosevelt that also included: "As you know, we are in urgent need of some of your older destroyers to tide us over the next few months. I well understand your difficulties, and I am certain that you will do your best to procure them for us before it is too late."

At this time, Britain was ordering 90 percent of its firearms, munitions, and explosives from the United States, and 95 percent of all American exports of airplanes and airplane parts were also being purchased by Britain. Between September 1939 and the end of 1940, the United States sold 132 merchant ships to Britain and 43 to Canada.

On July 20, President Roosevelt approved a bill authorizing a two-ocean Navy and providing for the construction of 200 warships, including seven battleships of 55,000 tons each. This defense program provided for an expenditure of $28 billion, or $12 billion less than the entire national debt.

On July 31, Churchill cabled Roosevelt: "It has now become most urgent for you to let us have the destroyers... for which we have asked... I am confident, now that you know exactly how we stand, that you will leave nothing undone to ensure that fifty or sixty of your oldest destroyers are sent to me at once. I can fit them very quickly with Asdics and use them against U-boats on the Western Approaches, and so keep the modern and better gunned craft for

Chapter Two

the Narrow Seas against invasion. Mr. President, with great respect I must tell you that in the long history of the world this is a thing to do NOW."

On August 20, at 11:00 a.m., the U.S. Commander of the Atlantic Squadron and his commander destroyers were ordered to report to the Chief of Naval Operations that afternoon. On the chance that the meeting would include the subject of the destroyers which Churchill had been requesting, they took along some preliminary plans, including lists of vessels for transfer that had been drawn up weeks before.

After 48 hours of conferences and telephone calls, the list of destroyers to be handed over to Britain was approved. This assignment was scheduled for September 6, 1940; Halifax, Nova Scotia would be the transfer site. The vessels would be transferred in groups of eight, every two weeks.

On August 27, Congress authorized induction of the National Guard into federal service. Four days later, the initial units were called out.

On August 30, the Chief of Naval Operations, or CNO, ordered by telephone to the commander destroyers, Atlantic Squadron, for the first eight destroyers to proceed to Boston and prepare for transfer.

On September 3, at 7:50 p.m., the Navy issued the first written instructions dealing with the transfer: "Proceed with project to turn over fifty destroyers to appropriate British authorities at Halifax in accordance with previous plan and tentative... instructions."

On September 4, the first destroyers sailed for Halifax and by September 6, all were anchored in Halifax Harbor, and *The Duchess of Richmond* entered the port with the first of the British crews for these ships.

The *St. Louis* and its aircraft continued to serve on neutrality patrol during this time: starting from Norfolk, the home port, then heading south toward South America, and continuing the triangle by heading to Bermuda. Next, the *St. Louis* headed back to Norfolk for several days for provisions, short liberties, fuel, etc. After refreshing its provisions, the *St. Louis* utilized the same route heading back — past Cape Hatteras, the Greater and Lesser Antilles — and approached the South American continent.

Occasionally, the *St. Louis* interacted with British ships like the cruiser HMS Caradoc (D60). These British ships sat on the same radio frequency as the *St. Louis*, thereby picking up the radio transmissions which declared the nationality of each of the ships which were reported to the U.S. Navy headquarters. United States destroyers had even convoyed British merchant ships during the North Atlantic run; in fact, USS Rueben James (DD 245) was sunk during this period and resulted in the loss of many great American Navy men. The *St. Louis* finally completed its neutrality runs, and soon thereafter was given the assignment of lend-lease.

At this point, the United States was fully committed to helping the British. The *St. Louis* visited each of the British possessions along the eastern seaboard, from South America all the way up to Newfoundland, and set up American air and naval bases. In return, the British navy received many of our World War I destroyers. The United States knew that excellent legal counsel was critical for such significant foreign interactions, so the U.S. Navy selected Rear Admiral Greenslade to support and oversee the effort. He arrived by air to the Norfolk Naval Base, where a flag was hoisted to yardarm for his arrival—by none other than USS St. Louis.

Chapter Two

Orders of the Day

Carry out the sea routine and the following:

0530   Call all idlers.

0600   Turn to. Set modified material condition baker-day. Scrub paint work. Clean and dry all waterways. Clean and shine brightwork in all boats. After decks are dried, break out all mooring lines and fake them down on the centerline as directed. Distribute large cylindrical care fenders as follows: one on the forecastle between turret one and two; one on each side amidships, and one on each side aft, just forward of the propeller guards. Distribute four ball fenders on the forecastle and two to the fifth division aft.

0815   Turn to. Shine all brightwork. Fake or flemish down all lines. Pipe down all clothes lines. Eliminate all Irish pennants. Get everything shipshape about the decks for entering port.

0830   Dump all trash and garbage. CPPO check on this.

0845   Set material condition baker on the third deck and below.

0900   Light off the incinerator. From this time until 10 miles from the Pacific end of the channel all garbage, trash, and boxes will be burned. Nothing but liquids will be dumped overboard. Metal cans will be retained on board.

0915   (About) Station the special sea details. Have jacobs ladder, boat lines, and fenders ready on the starboard side of the quarterdeck to receive pilot and boarding officer.

0945   (About) Sound "officers' call." Hold quarters for entering port and for muster.

0950   (About) Sound "assembly."

1000   (About) Pass through Colon breakwater entrance. Set modified material condition baker-day on the third deck and below. Rig both lifeboats inboard.

1100   (About) Moor to Gatun Lock pier using ownlines. Have cane fenders over; three on side toward pier; two on the other side. Receive wire lines from the electric locomotives; lead these lines at the bow through the forward-closed chocks on each side and secure on the forward outboard bitts. Aft, lead the wire lines through the stern-closed chocks and secure on the after quarter bitts. Unmoor when locomotives are ready to control the ship into the first lock. When directed, land the brow provided to disembark passengers and land mail.

1145 (About) Enter second Gatun Lock.

1230 (About) Enter third Gatun Lock.

1315 (About) Enter Gatun Lake. Hold general field day. Protect linoleum-covered and painted decks as usual. Scrub all hose and canvas. Scrub down all decks with sand. Sand and canvas all brightwood work. Thoroughly scrub all lower deck paintwork and linoleum-covered decks. Wax and re-polish decks.

1530 Wash and dry down all decks. Remove all traces of sand. Shine brightwork. Fake or flemish down all lines. Get everything shipshape about the decks.

1700 (About) Enter second lock.

1820 Proceed across Miraflores Lake.

1840 Moor to pier at Miraflores lock. Take locomotive's lines as before. Land the brow to exchange motion pictures programs.

1920 Leave Miraflores lock. Proceed to sea. Set material condition baker on the third deck and below.

2030 (About) Off the channel entrance, disembark the pilot. Motion pictures- "Yesterday's Hereos," with Robert Sterling and Jean Rogers.

Notes: (1) Working division—6th.
      (2) Uniform while in locks will be uniform of the day.

CC:	Capt., Exec. Off., all officers All Offices, CPPO, CPO Mess CCStd, Mess Treasurers, Exec. Off. for BB's and Div. PO's.	D. A. Spencer Commander, USN Executive Officer

Chapter Three

"My Acquaintance with Admiral Greenslade"
By Chris LaBonte

Before my Navy career, in my small home town of Bellevue, Ohio (population 8,000), I was a delivery boy on a local bread route after school. Unknown to me at the time, one of my customers was Rear Admiral Greenslade's mother.

One day I told her that I was going to join the Navy. She told me, "I think that is wonderful. My son is in the Navy. When he comes home, I will tell him that you are going into the Navy." One Saturday she said, "My son is home and I would like you to meet him." A mature man in civilian clothes came to the door. I was quite surprised since I expected a younger man. He told me that his mother said I was contemplating going into the Navy. He said that would be wonderful since it would be a very good experience and would do me good. We said our goodbyes and I left. He didn't mention at the time that he was an officer and neither had his mother.

In October 1938, I did join the Navy. I went through training in Rhode Island and was transferred to the USS New York for temporary duty while waiting for the *St. Louis* to be commissioned. We commissioned *St. Louis*- had our problems with the main engine room, and became known as "Two Screw Lou." We went on Neutrality Act patrol.

One day we received word that an admiral was going to come aboard and we were going to eight islands. He was going to inspect them for Naval bases and we would trade 50 United States destroyers for the bases. The day arrived and the Admiral was piped aboard. Suddenly I saw Mr. Greenslade looking like Lord Nelson in his full dress regalia complete with the gold echelons on his shoulders. To my amazement I realized that this was the man who had talked to me calmly about joining the Navy. I told some of the crew members about this and they were in favor of my saying to the admiral, "Here I am—remember me?" or at least take some of my hometown papers which I was receiving through the mail so he could also catch up with the hometown news. I felt I would be imposing on his rank so I did not do this.

The Admiral was aboard for quite some time. Finally he left our ship and eventually we went west with the *St. Louis*. We went to Hawaii—made a lot of drill runs preparing for WWII. Finally, we arrived at Mare Island Navy Yard. At that time, I heard of a ship going into commission named the *Washington* which I assumed was the battleship which was on the east coast. I volunteered and again was surprised to find it turned out to be the United States liner cruise ship *Washington*. To make a long story short, it was renamed the USS Mt. Vernon.

In the interim, Admiral Greenslade had become Vice Admiral and Commander of the Western Sea Frontier with headquarters at San Francisco. Quite some time later, when the *Mt. Vernon* was in San Francisco, the Admiral came aboard and inspected it since it was a troop-carrying ship. I still did not contact him.

After the war, at one of our Memorial Day Parades in Bellevue, Rear Admiral Greenslade and I participated in the parade and he gave the main speech at the cemetery. This particular time I did approach him and talked to him face to face. I asked him if he remembered the young man to whom he had given advice to go into the Navy (I had spent seven years in the service). I told him of the episodes of seeing him at different places but not contacting him. To my surprise he did remember me and was disappointed that I had not done so because he would have liked to help me in any way that he could. I told him that I felt it would be like asking special favors above my shipmates which is what I did not want. My wife took movies of him and I having our chat which I still have.

The Admiral died a few days before his 70th birthday in Bellevue.

Chapter Three

It was an honor for me to stand as an Honor Guard at his casket in Bellevue for the funeral services held there. He was then taken to Maryland to be buried with full honors at Annapolis, the academy he had graduated from in 1899.

To me, the Admiral was a soft-spoken, well-mannered, modest gentleman. He was friendly and unassuming, a man who did not play up his high rank. He was about 5 ft. 8 in. (about my height). I felt that he treated me and greeted me like a next door neighbor.

The Navy Mothers of Bellevue named their organization the "Admiral Greenslade Chapter." I am proud to say my mother was a member of this chapter.

* * * * * * * * * *

The destroyer-base exchange, in effect, marked the end of the American neutrality and moved the United States into "limited war." Significant in these actions was the fact that President Roosevelt had to bypass Congress and exercise executive authority. It was hoped that the Axis could be defeated without actual American participation.

Early in 1941 there was a major alert. Japanese appeared to be heading for Pearl. There were numerous ships at Pearl, including *St. Louis*. *St. Louis* launched aircraft before dawn to search for the potential enemy. The planes often flew approximately sixteen hours per day and night for several months—dive bombing and aerial gunnery runs.

The Japanese pressed for experiments to prepare for launching aerial torpedoes in the barely forty-foot-deep Pearl Harbor waters after the British Navy sank three Italian battleships in heavily fortified Taranto in November 1940. The British accomplished this with only twenty-one torpedo bombers, equipped with torpedoes fitted with wooden fins to prevent them from "porpoising" and hitting the shallow bottom. Until then, it was considered impossible to launch aerial torpedoes in water less than 75 feet deep.

In March 1941, the British authorities began breaking the German Naval codes, perfecting the art, and passing on the information to American cryptanalysts throughout World War II. Americans had broken the Japanese diplomatic code in the mid-1940's and were reading its secret messages as soon as transmitted.

St. Louis participated in fleet maneuvers and conducted patrols during the winter of 1940 and 1941, then steamed to California for an overhaul at Mare Island.

On May 27, 1941, Captain Rood took command of the light cruiser *St. Louis*, then in the Navy Yard at Mare Island, California.

Captain G.A. Rood, U.S. Navy

Captain G.A. Rood, U.S. Navy, who holds the Navy Cross for his brilliant command of the submarine L-1 in making a passage alone across the Atlantic in the winter, and for operations in the Irish Sea during World War I, graduated from the Naval Academy in June 1911. His first duty as a commissioned officer was aboard USS Mississippi (BB23) where he performed duties in gunnery, engineering, and signals. He was then ordered to the old cruiser USS Baltimore (C3) for a short period and then to the submarine tender USS Tonapah (BM8) for duties in navigation, gunnery, and training in submarines.

On May 19, 1913, Captain Rood began his submarine career

Chapter Three

aboard the submarine C-1 for duty in navigation, gunnery and engineering. He succeeded the C-1 with duties aboard the submarines C-2, C-3, and C-5, the latter of which Captain Rood commanded.

He was ordered to the old cruiser USS Columbia (C12), and after a short period there, ordered to his first tour of shore duty for instruction in diesel engines at New London, and then instruction in torpedoes in Newport. He was then ordered to command the submarine L-1 on April 17, 1916, and it was for the performance of his duties aboard this vessel that he was awarded the Navy Cross. He then reported aboard the transport USS Harrisburg (ID 1663) for a short period of duty; he was again ordered to a tour of shore duty, this time in Washington, D.C. on the submarine desk of the Bureau of Engineering, and returned to sea in command of the submarines 0-6 and 0-9.

Captain Rood again reported to Washington for a tour of shore duty in the Bureau of Engineering (submarine desk- electrical) in October 1918. His next sea duty was aboard the battleship USS Utah (BB31) as assistant gunnery officer and chief engineer. This duty lasted twenty-seven months after which the captain returned to shore duty as the inspector of engineering material (aviation) in New York.

He returned to submarine duty as commanding officer of the submarine USS Bass (V2) on January 19, 1925, which duties he performed for thirty-nine months. The captain was then ordered to Washington for another tour of shore duty in September 1928, with the Bureau of Navigation (records).

He served as the flag secretary of the battleships, Battle Force, for thirty-two months beginning on October 19, 1930. His next tour of shore duty was at the Naval Academy in the Department of Engineering in June 1933.

Captain Rood returned to sea as executive officer of the heavy cruiser USS Salt Lake City (CA25) and then was again called to Washington to the Division of Naval Intelligence for another tour of shore duty.

The captain had completed eighteen years of sea duty, was married, and the father to a daughter, 16, and a son, 14.

In May 1941, Commander Fink was transferred to *St. Louis*

as executive officer. In June 1942, Commander Fink completed twenty-four years commissioned service in the United States Navy and served seventeen years and eight months at sea.

Carl K. Fink, Commander, U.S. Navy

Comdr. Carl K. Fink, U.S. Navy, graduated from the U.S. Naval Academy in June 1918, during World War I. After a short period on board USS New Hampshire (BB70), he was ordered to duty on USS Alywin (DD47) in the war zone. He remained on this duty doing convoy work and patrolling the coasts of England and France until the Armistice in November 1918.

Returning to the United States in July 1919, he was ordered to USS Tingey (DD272), a destroyer built at the Squantum Plant of the Fore River Ship Building Company. In this vessel he was gunnery officer, torpedo officer, and first lieutenant and remained there until March 1920. At this time *Tingey* was in Honolulu, and Commander Fink was transferred to USS Rizal (DD174) as chief engineer. Shortly thereafter, *Rizal* sailed for the Asiatic Station. Duty on that station was performed on *Rizal*, USS Long (DD209), and USS John D. Edwards (DD216), the commander being the executive officer of the latter ship. In June 1922, he was transferred to USS Wilmington (PG8) as gunnery officer and senior watch officer to bring that vessel from the Asiatic Station to Portsmouth, New Hampshire. This voyage lasted until September 1922, when *Wilmington* arrived in Portsmouth having returned to the United States via Suez and the Mediterranean Sea. Upon arrival in the United States, he became executive officer of *Wilmington* and later the commanding officer. In February 1923, Commander Fink was ordered as navigator of USS Shawmut (CM4), the flagship of the Mine Force. He remained in this capacity until January 1926, when he was ordered to his first tour of shore duty, which was as officer in charge of the Branch Hydrographic Office at Cleveland, Ohio. While ashore, in April 1926, the commander was married.

Going back to sea in January 1928, he was ordered to USS Texas (BB35), flagship of the U.S. Fleet, as broadside division officer and senior watch officer. After serving a year and a half in this capacity,

Chapter Three

he became senior assistant engineer until the completion of that cruise in January 1931.

From February 1931, until May 1933, he had shore duty in the Bureau of Navigation in the Navy Department.

He was next ordered to sea in May 1933, as communication officer of USS Saratoga (CV3), and remained there until June 1935, at which time he was transferred to USS Babbitt (DD128) as commanding officer.

He was in command of *Babbitt* until June 1936, when he was ordered to shore duty as an assistant professor in naval science and tactics with the Naval ROTC unit at Northwestern University in Evanston, Illinois.

This shore duty ended in June 1938, and the commander was ordered as navigator of USS Arizona (BB39). In December 1938, he was selected for the rank of commander, and in May 1939, was transferred to the staff of the Commander Base Force as fleet personnel officer. His office at that time was in USS Argonne (AS10), and during the two years he served as fleet personnel officer, he served under Admiral Watts, Meyers, and Calhoun.

St. Louis left Mare Island after a short period and headed back to Pearl Harbor, arriving there on June 20, 1941, and resumed operations in Hawaiian waters.

It appeared that Captain Rood immediately impressed the crew with his ship handling. They recalled one occasion during maneuvers with other ships, aircraft, and subs, when Abe Dietz was told to report to the bridge since he had experience in aircraft and radio shack procedure. He copied the coded communications from the aircraft, subs, and ships, and handed it to the communication (intelligence) officer for decoding. At one point, one of the U.S. subs surfaced at approximately a 45 degree angle to starboard at several hundred yards ahead of *St. Louis*. Captain Rood ordered the helmsman "port 20 degrees," and thus may have avoided an ugly situation.

At one of the particularly hazardous recoveries at sea, with seas running heavy, all aircraft were finally taken aboard safely. Suddenly, the crew was surprised to see Captain Rood walking aft, coming to each of the men who flew, calling each of them by name, and saying "well done." He was a great and very human person.

War in the Pacific was expected momentarily by many after the end of July 1941. It is evident here in a letter written by Abe Dietz of Santa Monica, California, to his folks:

July 25, 1941

I don't suppose you've wondered why I hadn't written any sooner or why I don't write more often than I do—I'm certain you are fairly well familiar with conditions at present—at least you'll believe we are beyond a doubt undergoing the toughest routine and most rugged conditions that the Navy has had to contend with for many years. To you people at home it must appear puzzling to wonder what we do out here. I cannot go into any sort of detail describing the various phases of our day's duties or our military maneuvers—suffice it to say that we are at present in the most critical stage since the last war and that at any moment the catastrophe may strike—and in order to prepare ourselves for every sort of condition that may be encountered later on, we are working days and nights so that we will not be caught napping. In my opinion the fleet is in the best condition of readiness that it has ever been in, and I'm glad of that. We've been at sea for some time now operating under actual war conditions so that in case of war, every man will be ready and few changes will be necessary. At night we operate with ships completely darkened, so that I haven't seen a movie in so long, I don't think I can remember what one is like. Flight operations are held so regular, in the past ten days it seems I've spent more time in the air than I have aboard ship—poor weather or rough seas, nothing holds us back these days—we just go right along, catapulting the planes several times a day from early morning, come in to refuel and for a snack and then off again. Usually on a long navigation hop of several hundred miles, I cuddle up in the rear cockpit for short periods and catch a few winks—we get so little of that aboard ship. On many occasions we've had some mighty rough experiences returning aboard ship—catapulting a plane from the ship may appear hazardous, but coming back to the ship, scooped up by the sea sled and hoisted aboard is even worse. For about 100 seconds everything hangs in the balance; that is, from

Chapter Three

the moment the plane hits the water, speeds after the sea sled, hooks onto it properly, and is hoisted aboard, anything can happen. It's the most exciting part of flying, and once in a long while something may happen. What I was leading up to is the fact that a few weeks ago I was involved in one of these messes during some unusually rough seas and while attempting a recovery maneuver, the plane was wrecked, capsized in the broad Pacific with the pilot and myself up to our necks in salt water. The ship was far in the distance in nothing flat, and we seemed so alone in the world. In a short while, however, the crash boat was out there to pick us up, with neither of us the worse for our experience. As a matter of fact the doctor gave us a good shot of brandy to remove the chills and cheer us up a bit.

* * * * * * * * * *

In August 1941, *St. Louis* sailed west with other cruisers of the Battle Force; it patrolled between Wake, Midway, and Guam, then proceeded to Manila, whence she returned to Hawaii at the end of September. On the 28th of September, she entered the Pearl Harbor Navy Yard for upkeep, and on December 7, she was moored to the pier in Southeast Lock.

One of the major achievements of the gun crews of *St. Louis* was the "clean sweep," made by all five turrets and four mounts, at the short range practice fired in October 1941.

St. Louis was the only ship in the fleet to attain this record for the current gunnery year.

Every member of the gun crew was paid $10.00 in prize money and authorized to wear the Navy "E" for "excellence in gunnery" on their uniforms. Painting of the coveted "E" on the outside of the turrets and mounts was discontinued because of camouflage regulations. Another *St. Louis* job!

In November 1941, a minor incident created the onset of sharp and bitter criticism regarding *St. Louis*, which echoed and reechoed in the halls of Congress and throughout the nation. Versions of the story have appeared in many publications throughout the years. Some accounts report a sea battle in the China Seas during *St. Louis'* brief visit to Manila in which The Lou—supposedly accompanied by British warships—sank a German raider.

Al Seton recalled the consequences of this incident aboard The Lou. One night at sea, late in November 1941, Al stepped into the passage going forward to "officers country" at about 2200 hours. Standing outside the Captain's office in his immaculate CPO dress blues was the captain's writer.

"Special liberty tonight, chief?" Al asked as they steamed at sea, a hundred miles from the nearest liberty port.

"I wish it was," he replied. "The captain's going to hold 'captain's mast' in his cabin. I'm waiting for him to buzz to say he's ready. The Chief Master at Arms will take a seaman right on up when I give him the word the captain is ready."

"Special captain's mast?" Al asked. "Why?" "Here, take a look at this letter but keep it quiet," he said, handing Al a letter directly to the commanding officer of USS St. Louis. The letter was from the Secretary of the Navy, asking for the commanding officer to investigate and report action taken; enclosed was a copy of the letter from the ship's seaman—the letter which was causing such a stir in Congress and in the United States.

"Wow!" Al exclaimed. "Portsmouth for him!"—that's the Navy equivalent to "off with their heads."

Sometime later, the captain's writer stopped by the gunnery office, exclaiming in disbelief, "I still don't believe it. I've never seen a captain's mast quite like this one."

"Why, what happened, Chief?"

"Don't tell anyone, but when we assembled in the captain's cabin, Captain Rood turned to the seaman and asked: 'Son, did you write this letter?' while handing him a copy of his letter enclosed within the letter from the Secretary of the Navy."

"Seaman: 'Yes sir.'"

"Captain Rood: 'Son, have you ever thought of becoming a writer?'"

"Seaman: 'No sir.'"

"Captain Rood: 'Well son, you should. You write well and you have a wonderful imagination. Think about becoming a writer. That's all. Goodnight.' Captain Rood then turned to his desk and

Chapter Three

went to work on his incoming mail basket."

"I don't know what the captain is going to write to the Secretary of the Navy," the captain's writer wondered aloud, before turning to go aft to the CPO quarters.

The doctrines of Alexander de Seversky and Giulio Douhet, the Italian prophet of victory through air power, were exciting stimuli in the summer of 1941, and the theorists of strategic air warfare found ready markets for their views. Even professional judgment and long military experience were not immune to the newfound enthusiasm. Army General Marshall, in a background secret press briefing for some seven Washington correspondents on November 15, 1941 (three weeks before the Pearl Harbor attack), epitomized the misjudgments of the time.

He noted that the war with Japan was imminent, but he felt the United States' position in the Philippines was highly favorable. Our strength in the islands, he said, was far larger than the Japanese imagined. We were preparing not only to defend the Philippines, but to conduct an aerial offensive from these islands against Japan. Thirty-five B-17 Flying Fortresses were based in the Philippines—the greatest concentration of heavy bomber strength anywhere in the world. More planes were being sent to the islands, as were tanks and guns; the Philippines were being reinforced daily. If war did start, the B-17's would immediately attack the enemy's naval bases and would set the "paper" cities of Japan on fire. Although the B-17 did not have enough range to reach Japan and return to Philippine bases, General Marshall—with a political naiveté characteristic of many of our military men at the time—said optimistically that the bombers could continue on to Russian Vladivostok and would carry out shuttle bombing raids from Vladivostok and Philippine territory.

The new Convair B-24 bombers would soon be in production, General Marshall said, and these planes would be able to fly higher than any Japanese interceptors.

The General summed up the current Army optimism in one of the most amazingly mistaken appraisals of history. By about mid-December, he said, the War Department would feel rather secure in the Philippines. Flying weather over Japan was good; our high-flying bombers could quickly wreak havoc. If a Pacific war started, there would not be much need for our Navy; the U.S. bombers could spearhead a victory offensive virtually single-handed, or to paraphrase General Marshall's words, without the use of our shipping. Our own Pacific Fleet would stay out of range of Japanese air power in Hawaii.

General Marshall's optimism—induced by MacArthur, Commander of the U.S. Army Forces Far East, and Henry "Hap" Arnold's enthusiasm, Chief of the Army Air Forces—grew too, from the fertile soil of ignorance then generally shared in the Army; the ignorance of what air power meant, a lack of understanding of maritime power, and an astigmatic appreciation of the Japanese.

Yet it was already too little and too late. When the Japanese struck on December 7, 1941, there were only two operational radar sets in the Philippine Islands, thirty-five heavy bombers, and probably no more than sixty operational first-line fighters. The ten reserve divisions of the Philippine Army had been partially mobilized. There were more than 100,000 Filipinos in some kind of uniform, but most of them knew little and cared less about the mechanics of warfare. U.S. Army Troops numbered 31, 095 on November 30, including almost 12,000 Philippine scouts, an elite and well-trained special part of the regular army (Philippine-enlisted men, officered chiefly by Americans).

However, the Navy Department, which did not share the War Department's optimism about the defensibility of the Philippines, could promise no reinforcements for the Asiatic Fleet. As late as November 20, the Navy Department ordered Admiral Thomas C. Hart, its "small, taut, wiry, and irascible" commander, to carry out the pre-planned deployment of his fleet southward as the war plan required, rather than concentrate in Manila Bay as Admiral Hart had suggested.

Admiral Hart knew, as did General MacArthur, that no relief was anticipated for the Philippines until the U.S. Pacific fleet had made a step-by-step advance through the Caroline and Marshall Islands and had seized an advanced base at Truk. This concept was embodied in the "Rainbow 5" plan, a global plan worked out in conformity with the British which anticipated war by the United States with both Germany and Japan, thus updating the obsolescent

Chapter Three

"Orange 1" ocean-war plan. Rainbow 5, which grew out of staff talks between the United States and Britain in January, February, and March 1941, and was completed shortly before Pearl Harbor, clearly called for a defensive strategy in the Pacific and implicitly, at least, "accepted... the loss of the Philippines, Guam, and Wake." It stated initially that the United States did not expect to add to its military strength in the Far East, but a revision in November 1941—the product of the new and optimistic Army attitude in Washington and Manila—authorized offensive air operations "in furtherance of the strategic defensive."

"Words Once Spoken Can Never Be Recalled" Navy Yard, Pearl Harbor, T.H.

Orders of the Day
Sunday, December 7, 1941

Carry out the port routine, guard mail trips, boat schedule, and the following:

0545	Send 6-hand working party to the dock for ice; Cook, SC4c in charge.
0600	Reveille.
0630	Turn to. Clean sweep and clamp down all decks. Boat crews turn to.
0715	Send 4-hand working part in MWB with brooms, buckets, and scrubbers to fleet landing; Boyence, Cox, 1st Div. in charge.
0800	Hoist military guard and medical guard flags.
0800	Turn to. Continue with the ship's work. Make all gear shipshape about the ship. Muster on stations and make the reports thereof promptly to the executive officer's office.
0815	Send Catholic Church party to receiving barracks. Uniform-undress whites with neckerchiefs.
0830	Land the starboard watch shore patrol consisting of: Linton, BM1c, Clendenen, CM1c, Curl, R.H. GM2c, and Hart, MM2c.
0830	Liberty for the port watch to expire at 0730 on board for chief petty officers, and petty officers first class, and at 0100, Monday, December 8, 1941, for all other ratings.
0930	Knock off work. Holiday routine. All hands shift into clean uniform of the day. Keep the ship, boats, brow and accommodation ladder neat. Keep all hands in clean uniform of the day. Sun bathing from 0930-1130.
1000	Send Protestant Church party to receiving barracks. Uniform-undress whites with neckerchiefs.
1245	Send Monroe, RM3c to Aiea Club House Landing as beach guard until 1800. (Save supper for Monroe).

Chapter Three

P.M. Holiday routine. Sun bathing from 1300 to 1700.
1920   Movies: "When Ladies Meet" starring Joan Crawford, Robert Taylor, Greer, Garson.
Notes: (1) Duty head of department and security officer- Lt. Cmdr. Gill.
(2) Duty section- 1st; standby- 3rd.
(3) Working division- 1st.
(4) Running boats- #1ML, MB, and #1MWB.

C.K. Fink
Commander, U.S. Navy,
Executive Officer

Chapter Four

An Eyewitness Report Etched in Memory:
St. Louis at Pearl Harbor

By Norman J. Heine, Ex-USN

December 7, 1941, started as any other Sunday morning on board USS St. Louis. Bud and I were waiting for the motor launch that would take us to morning services. We were "plank owners" along with many of the crew, having been aboard the light cruiser since she was commissioned in 1939.

Though our home port was San Pedro, we had operated out of Pearl Harbor since 1940. Weekends in port usually meant a wing-ding of a Saturday night followed by a quiet day recuperating at the beach on Sunday.

Bud stuck two extra packs of cigarettes in his sock, planning on a full day off the ship. There was no way we could foresee that a sniping invader would foul up our plans for a relaxed liberty.

A steady humming sound exploded into a roar. On the horizon we spotted planes thundering toward the island.

"Why the hell is the Army flying on a Sunday?" Bud blurted out. He leaned against the rail, curious but not too concerned about the approaching planes.

Suddenly, an oblong object plunged from the bottom of each of the planes, and streaked down toward Battleship Row. As the lead plane banked for a turn, the wing bared the stark outline of the

Chapter Four

Rising Sun.

"My God! Those are Japanese planes!" someone screamed out the startling news.

Just then the motor launch pulled up alongside the ship to pick up the last of the stragglers for church, namely Bud, myself, and about ten others.

"Get the hell outta' here!" we yelled a warning to the boatswain. For a minute he peered up at us, unable to believe what he heard. Then with a quick twist of the tiller, he swung the launch back toward land.

Out of nowhere, the enemy appeared, aiming straight for the defenseless boat. Machine gun bullets peppered the small launch. Desperately the boatswain tried to escape the onslaught. It was our initiation to the brutalities of war. The boatswain's motionless figure draped over the tiller, the jumper of his whites almost completely stained red, his blood spilling from his wounds.

"Madre de Dios!" I heard Manuel, one of gunners, mutter the prayer as he blessed himself several times. The tone of his voice sure sounded different. He usually turned to his native tongue only when he was angry.

The general quarters warning blared out, jerking us to action. "Man your battle stations! Man your battle stations! This is not a drill!"

What had been a routine call on maneuvers took on a desperate urgency. We all scrambled to our stations, disbelief on every face as the "bong, bong!" repeated the warning over the loudspeaker.

With the engine rooms not ready for steaming, some of us machinists were rushed to quarters to clip 50-caliber ammunition into belts for the machine guns.

At first, only tracer ammunition was available. This particular shell leaves a white stream as it is fired and lets the gunner know how accurate his aim is. It explodes immediately on contact.

"Get the key from the chief in charge of the small arms locker. We need the armor-piercing shells!" Before the young officer's order could be carried out, a 1st class grabbed a pair of bolt cutters and snapped the lock off the door.

"No time to wait for any key, sir!" The 1st class was not

disrespectful, just practical. There was no time to waste. Without another word, the lieutenant joined the non-com in handing out the more powerful ammunition. Rank was forgotten.

As the name indicates, the armor-piercing shells make contact, penetrating through the metal of a plane before exploding. Some of the men working on the machine gun belts, including Bud and myself, were green. But within a few minutes we were keeping up with the best of them.

Meanwhile, topside, the men moved fast as orders were shouted.

"Anchor those 50-calibers in place!" The ten machine guns, five on the port side and five on the starboard side, the one-point-one on the upper deck and the 5-inch anti-aircraft guns were already lashing out at the enemy. These guns alone were credited with three "probable" downings of Japanese planes. With the circuit breakers ashore for repair, the gunners operated the batteries manually.

There were five 6-inch turrets with three guns in each turret manned and standing by. These particular guns were not designed for anti-aircraft action. We were not sure they would be used, but they were ready.

Men on the 5-inchers had a wraparound steel protection. The gunners on the 50-caliber machine guns had only helmets of World War I vintage to protect them from the machine gun fire the enemy planes were spitting out.

From the beginning of the year through July we had been on maneuvers, so after the first shock wore off, routine took over.

When we first pulled into the harbor on Friday, the 5th of December, we were ordered to the Navy Yard for an overhaul. USS Helena (CL50) took over our berth in the harbor and we tied alongside *Honolulu*. We grumbled plenty when we were told to keep one boiler hot to furnish our own auxiliary power for the various electrical equipment aboard. *Honolulu*, being the flagship of Cruiser Combat 9, would receive her power from the dock.

It was late Friday when we finally tied up. We were all glad to hear the order to wait until Monday to remove the ammunition from the ship. So it happened that on this fateful Sunday, we were armed to the teeth with one boiler already hot.

This day *St. Louis* would really earn the "E" we were rated during spring gunnery exercises. Our targets were shooting back at us and they were hell-bent on blasting everything in sight.

Ships in the harbor with their ammunition removed had nothing with which to fight. Helpless to defend themselves, they were like sitting ducks. Wave after wave of attacking planes dropped their deadly loads.

Several men on one of the unarmed ships desperately threw potatoes at the low-flying planes. What a pitiful effort! Witnessing scenes like that caused the change from a happy-go-lucky peacetime gob to a cold, hard, combat sailor.

Men were running in all directions, each with a job to do. One machinist of slight stature who was working with us grabbed a completed belt and, swinging the heavy belt over his shoulder, ran up the ladder—a feat that he was unable to duplicate later under normal conditions. As he reached the top of the ladder, he stepped right into the path of the captain, knocking the officer to the deck.

"Embarrassed as hell," the machinist told us later. "I helped the skipper to his feet and proceeded to brush off his uniform."

"Where were you heading with that belt, sailor?" The captain asked.

"To the nearest gun that needs it, sir."

"Well, get going. You should have knocked me out for getting in your way."

Many years later, he and the captain had a hearty laugh over the incident, but at the time, they saw no humor in it.

Suddenly, one of the 50-caliber guns broke loose from the deck, knocked the sailor who was operating it completely out and started hopping down the deck. The trigger froze and the gun was shooting in all directions.

"Grab it!" one sailor shouted.

"Not me! You grab it, if you're crazy enough!" a second sailor yelled back. They chased the runaway gun down the deck and it finally stopped firing, landing on the hangar deck. Quickly, they carried it back to position and anchored it firmly in place. Minutes later, the gun was back on duty with an operator aiming it the right way.

Each time I came up on the deck with a completed belt, I could hardly believe the destruction going on. Large billows of smoke

The Saga of the Lucky Lou

poured into the sky from Hickam Field to the left of *St. Louis*, blackening the same sky that had been clear and cloudless a short time before.

"All machinists report to the engine room on the double!"

"It's about time!" I thought. I found out later that though it seemed longer, actually only 20 minutes had passed since the first bomb exploded.

As we rushed to our more familiar station, a tremendous explosion shook *St. Louis* from stem to stern.

"Damage control party, check aft!" a command blared out. Just as we reached the engine room, we heard the repeat: "No damage aft, sir!"

Once down the ladder, we learned that a 500-pound bomb had hit the dock, knocking *Honolulu* and *St. Louis* together, smashing and sinking two motor launches that were tied up between the ships. Thank God no men were in the small boats. They wouldn't have had a chance.

"We've got a head start with one boiler hot," the chief machinist's mate reminded us. "Let's move!"

The crew in the boiler operating space took auxiliary steam, bled it into the other seven boilers, and within an hour all boilers were up to a full working capacity.

It was almost 0930 when the chief notified the skipper we had a full head of steam. At 0931 the captain snapped out the order: "Full speed astern."

The deck force grabbed the nearest fire ax and chopped us loose from the dock. We cleared the harbor with all anti-aircraft guns blazing. Eyewitnesses later commented that it was an impressive and never-to-be-forgotten sight to see *St. Louis* head for sea with all her guns spitting fire. We left the dock in such a hurry that we hit bottom with one of our screws. It was so badly bent that it had to be quickly secured and we went full speed ahead on three screws.

Back in the boiler room the firemen worked feverishly. Suddenly an excited deckhand burst in with an alarming report.

"Black smoke! Black smoke pouring out of number two stack!" he yelled to the chief. Before anything could be checked, a young officer came in.

Chapter Four

"Keep up the black smoke! I don't know what the hell caused it, but it's a perfect smoke screen for *Phoenix*!" The cruiser *Phoenix* had none of her guns in commission at the time.

But this smoke screen had not been planned. What had caused it?

When changing speeds from time to time, the firemen in the boiler operating space put larger sprayer tips on the plates that inject the fuel oil into the burners. This keeps up a full head of steam. A chart posted in the master engine room has all information as to what tip goes in, depending on speed and steam pressure. Someone in the operating space put a sprayer plate in the boiler without a tip. Instead of a thin spray into the burner, it was a solid stream of oil causing number two stack to pour the heavy black smoke.

Some observers thought that this was done intentionally, but no orders had been given to that effect. Some thought *St. Louis* was on fire, but we were not damaged. Had this occurred during peacetime, the guilty party would have been severely reprimanded. All I could think was: "What a lucky break for USS Phoenix!"

As we swung around Ford Island, which was strictly Navy air, we sighted the hangars belching fire and black smoke. How badly had our planes been damaged? Were there any left in condition to fight off another attack? We couldn't tell the extent of the destruction.

St. Louis steamed along at 25 knots, maneuvering around the wounded USS Nevada which had run aground to keep from capsizing. What a beating they had taken!

A sudden frantic shout from one of the deckhands struck terror in the hearts of all of us who heard him.

"Torpedo! Torpedo!" he pointed out over the starboard bow. Those on deck could see the wake of the dreaded enemy fish. I had just come topside for some needed equipment and took a quick look at the enemy missile speeding toward *St. Louis*.

It didn't take much thought to figure out their object in launching the torpedo at that spot. To sink us in the channel would block the passage completely. Their first attempt with *Nevada* had failed. Now the midget sub aimed for the cruiser.

We were unable to change course. We had no alternative but to keep heading out. Orders were shouted through the address system.

The light cruiser zigzagged like a "drunken sailor" in a desperate effort to escape. But the path of the torpedo was straight and true.

Suddenly, a muffled impact exploded into a mountain of water as a hidden coral reef lent itself to our defense. Quick action by the radioman located the sniper sub. Now it was our turn.

A determined gunner took careful aim with one of the 5-inch guns, lowering it to water level. One burst of fire. Then a shout as the smoke cleared and the damaged conning tower of the two-man sub bobbed to the surface. No longer able to operate, the sub was eventually captured.

It was natural to believe that the attacking planes were being sent out from a Japanese aircraft carrier. Our captain requested permission to go after the carrier, but we were ordered to circle the island and protect it.

We welcomed Sunday dinner as a break from the tension. Since most of the mess crew including some of the cooks were on gun crews, the chief yeoman was in charge of the cooking.

"Hey, chief, these beans are only half-cooked!" Griping was a sure sign that the crew was back in form.

"Holy Samoleons! This is fightin' food?" Now that could only be Bud. We had lost track of each other during the heavy action, but I knew he'd never pass up chow, no matter who cooked it.

After griping together for a few minutes, we left the mess and joined a special detail. According to Navy Regulations, during wartime in a combat zone no naval vessel is allowed to have inflammable supplies aboard. "Strip the ship for action" it's called. It was a lighthearted task as the crew tossed all the cases of paint and metal polish over the side. We jokingly guessed the hours of labor we were eliminating as the sweat rolled off our bodies.

While patrolling late that afternoon, we spotted more planes approaching. Again the dreaded cry.

"Man your battle stations!"

The gunners took aim and waited for the planes to get in range.

"Hold your fire! These are our planes!" Naked relief replaced concern on the men's faces now that our planes were in the air.

For three days we cruised the area, always on the alert for the enemy. *St. Louis* was equipped with sonar sounding gear to detect

Chapter Four

enemy submarines. New radar equipment that would reveal any enemy surface craft was still in the process of being installed. Any and all sounds that we picked up brought the crew to battle stations on the double. For the three days, we had little sleep though we met no enemy.

Finally, we received orders to return to the inside of the harbor. Seeing the destruction close up actually made us sick to the stomach. We found that USS Helena had the hell shot out of the forward engine room while tied up in our berth.

Chipped paint on our 6-inch turrets from machine gun bullets fired by the enemy planes were mute evidence of how close they had come. We were damn lucky to have no casualties or no serious injuries in spite of all the action in which we took part.

For their valiant contribution at Pearl Harbor, the crew of USS St. Louis were awarded the first of eleven battle stars on the Asiatic-Pacific Area Service Medal. It was over 30 years ago that about 900 sailors, both non-coms and officers, shared this hellish experience on the light cruiser. Parts of the day's activities are vague, but the events described above are as vivid as if they happened yesterday.

Retired Rear Admiral George Arthur Rood was the captain of the Lucky Lou, as the ship was affectionately known from that day on. The Admiral kept in touch with many of us crewmembers through the Pearl Harbor Survivors' Association of which he was a member. On 30 March 1971, at the age of 82, the skipper died.

"He was a grand 'Old Man' and his passing will leave a gaping hole in the hearts of those who had the privilege of serving under him," commented Bill Misner, past president of San Gabriel PHSA and also a former *St. Louis* crewmember. "I know I will never think of Pearl Harbor without thinking of him and being grateful to him for just being there to guide us."

The words of one of the officers still ring out loud and clear:
"They'll remember *St. Louis*, men! They tasted our fire!"

Excerpted from All Hands Magazine, December 1973. Reprinted with permission.

St. Louis **In Action**

The Japs gave the signal,
Pearl Harbor rolled the ball.
The *St. Louis* went into action,
And their planes began to fall.
We headed down the channel,
In the middle of the fight,
And God was there to guide us,
And told us we were right.
He helped us in Pearl Harbor,
And helped us far at sea.
He put us on a course to steer,
The Road to Victory!

—Krauss.

Chapter Five

As Others Saw It That Day in Infamy

By Joseph A. Grodecki

My first battle: December 7, 1941. Time: 3:30 a.m. Was awakened to stand a cold iron watch in the forward engine room. Cold iron watch means that nothing in the forward engine room is running. I am only there to keep unauthorized personnel out and to prevent sabotage as we lay to the starboard side of USS Honolulu at Pier B-17 Pearl Harbor Navy Yard.

Time: 7:30 a.m. Relieved of my watch to eat breakfast and shower up for liberty at 0800.

Time: 7:55 a.m. Entering shower room in shorts with a towel over my shoulder, cigar box with toilet articles in my right hand and soap dish in my left hand. Just as I enter the shower room, a sailor came rushing out and bumped me hard enough to knock the cigar box out of my hand and spill all contents on the deck. I said: "Where in the hell is the fire, Mac?" With bewildered eyes and a hastened voice, he said: "Fire hell, we're being attacked!"

As I gathered my belongings from the deck, I heard a distant thunder. As I looked toward the porthole, I could see it was a sunny day. I immediately went for the porthole to look out. I saw a gray airplane with a red disk painted on the fuselage. It appeared first just forward on the port side of the USS Honolulu, then disappeared again behind the hull of the *Honolulu*. The plane was coming in very slowly and deliberately as if a training pilot was practicing a landing.

Suddenly, the airplane engine roared and made a steep right turning climb. I could see torpedo wake in the water heading straight for the USS Arizona. She already was hit, burning and smoking badly. It was the thunder I heard before.

The boatswains mate with his pipe came on the intercom system: "All hands man your battle stations. This is not a drill. I repeat, this is not a drill. It's the real mccoy—on the double."

I immediately went for the forward engine room. For the next one hour and fifty minutes I saw nothing. But I heard a lot of explosions as we prepared to get underway. With confidence, I was sure we would win for that day.

Three days later, upon entering Pearl Harbor with all that destruction, smoke, and fire still going on six battlewagons on the bottom of the bay, the dead being hauled away to be placed on the dock of Aiea Landing...

Confidence drained away. Despair entered as we stood at attention at our quarters, and upon looking at Aiea Landing, my knees turned weak and rubbery and could hardly support my weight. With super grit and determination I tried to straighten them out. My arms, hanging from my shoulders, were so weak that I don't believe I could have saluted if I wanted to. The sight was more than a twenty-year-old boy could bear. Tilting my head to look at a small white cloud drifting slowly by in the sky, I tried not to make it look obvious as to what was on my mind to the other crew members, but I am sure others had the same thought as mine... "thank God I am alive."

By Ray Peevey

We were tied alongside USS Honolulu that Sunday morning. I had a buddy on *Honolulu* and I was on his ship wrapping a present to send to my dad for Christmas. After I got the present wrapped, I went back to *St. Louis* to wait for my liberty card. We were going ashore together that day and I was going to mail my present. While I was waiting for my liberty card, general quarters sounded and we all went to our battle stations. I remember they said: "All hands, man your battle stations on the double. This is not a drill." I was in 6" turret number one. We went out looking for the Japanese fleet for

Chapter Five

three days and when we returned, they were still burying the dead. Boatload after boatload. My buddy's ship was hit and went back to the States for repairs so he mailed my present to my dad for me. I remember before we got underway, I looked out and saw ships sunk and burning everywhere. Men were jumping over the sides of a lot of the ships, right into oil burning on the water. I'll never forget it as long as I live.

By Owen S. Davies

I was dressing to go into Honolulu when the attack by the Japanese began. At first I thought that the explosions were merely routine blasting on Red Hill in preparation for fuel storage tanks. Then the general quarters alarm sounded with the words "All hands to battle stations. This is no drill." My GQ station was in the crypto room—my first impression of damage to the fleet units, devastating, and I am sure demoralizing to all hands.

I was concerned about my wife and five-year-old son whom I thought were en route from Long Beach to Honolulu via the SS Matsonia.

The most memorable persons aboard the ship to me that morning were the young untested crews of the 20 and 40 MM anti-aircraft batteries valiantly under fire. Our courageous Captain Rood got his ship underway, while the USS Nevada was getting pinned down partially across the channel by enemy bombs just moments ahead of us; *St. Louis* came close to going aground. Luckily, the screws only churned up the mud! Then, as if predestined to be sunk, a midget sub fired two torpedoes at us as we exited the channel. I heard over the phone in the crypto room, the lookout yell: "Here comes a torpedo toward our starboard beam! Here comes another torpedo!" There was a moment of silence then two explosions, muffled. The torpedoes had been set too deep and apparently exploded against the dredged-up coral before reaching the ship. The engineman (name not known) reportedly singlehandedly replaced a reproduction gear cover which usually took two or three men to lift off. This action was necessary to the ship's readiness for sea. And finally, there was the gunner's mate who had his legs amputated in the turret-breach well when the guns were suddenly elevated.

By Charles T. Patterson

I was bugler at the time, and was waiting for colors to take place when I saw the first plane drop a torpedo.

By R.W. Cameron

I was at my locker when general quarters sounded. I was in the handling room of turret two, and right after that was sent to the comm deck to get sound-powered phones as they had all been picked up for maintenance and repair. That's when I saw the first planes and the first of the bombing.

By Henry E. Von Genk Jr.

On December 7, 1941, I was sort of a free agent that day. My battle station was the port catapult, but that was a useless assignment that day, so I was a rubberneck for the first thirty minutes or so… I sure had a ringside seat to watch the Japanese planes torpedo the battleships. After a while I drifted forward towards turret four and the 50-caliber machine guns. The 50-cal crews never bothered to put water in the barrel water jackets nor secured the mounts to the deck. Therefore, the guns jumped all over the place as they fired, the barrels burned out rapidly, and the projectiles cork-screwed as they went through the air. While I was there, and officer manned a set of phones and was standing on the starboard side near turret five. One of the port 50-caliber mounts fell over on its trigger and sprayed a few rounds under turret five; one round put a knick in the left 6" gun barrel. Immediately after, I looked back at the officer on the phone to see how he was and all that was left was the phone on the deck. I guess the officer figured discretion was the better part of valor. Clipped 50-caliber ammo was running low, so I checked the clipping room and found three ship's cooks in there. I got some 50-cal ammo for them to clip. To get the ammo, I had to pass through the

Chapter Five

mess decks, through the wardroom, and down the trunk umpteen decks to the ammo magazine. While passing through the mess deck, I ran across a shipfitter messing around trying to seal a hole on the port side where an overboard discharge valve had been removed for repairs. The 5" or 6" hole was just above the water line. I couldn't convince him to get cracking on the job because he didn't believe me when I told him what was going on. As I passed through the wardroom, I saw that many breakfasts had been interrupted. You can believe that I snacked each time I passed through. I don't know how many boxes of ammo I carried. I was in the mess deck when a bomb went off between *Honolulu* and the pier. Man, did that shipfitter speed up his work after that. During one of my trips to the clipping room, I witnessed the Japanese bomb battleship row from a level flight. I did not see *Arizona* blow up though. On another trip I saw *Nevada* steam by toward the channel with the stern flag flying. When the word was passed that we were getting underway, I helped chop the lines that bound up to *Honolulu*. That was very interesting. Our 5" mounts were firing. *Honolulu's* 5" guns were also firing and it was very noisy. In addition to the manila lines, there were some welding leads from the pier across *Honolulu* going into the gun mounts and into our various hatches. I had a hammer, and would lay the welding lead onto the edge of the waterway and beat on it to sever it. I had cut quite a few until I got up to the welding lead that went into the hot case chute of the forward port 5" mount. As I started to cut it, the first lieutenant of *Honolulu*, who was standing on his ship's deck, stopped me and ordered me to pull the lead out of the mount and throw it over. I tugged on the lead while dodging hot cases and it wouldn't come out. I then cut the lead and threw the bitter end over at the feet of the first lieutenant. Man, was he mad. We had chopped all the lines and leads so we started pulling away, and somehow we got the word to strip the ship for action. To us, that meant getting rid of all useless wooden items, so we threw all the swabs, brooms, and their racks over the side. I went back to carrying ammo and was in the mess decks when the word was passed to standby for torpedoes to starboard; we were to either lie on the deck or bend at the knees to lessen injury. I heard later that these torpedoes struck a reef or something. I know they didn't hit us. The next

The Saga of the Lucky Lou

time I came topside, we were out of the harbor and at sea.

A bullet had penetrated our stern and was found on a stringer by one of the aviation division men. He was showing it to me when Ens. "Tiger" Tieg took it to show to Captain Rood. I don't know what happened to it. One bullet severed a strand of my port catapult launching cable and we had to change the cable. I heard, but never checked, that a bullet had penetrated one of our search lights up near the stacks.

As you know, we had only a peacetime crew on board when the war started, and to my knowledge we had never gone to Condition 2 or 3 between December 7th or 10th. I wound up standing four hours lookout, and then four hours off. That is neither Condition 2 or 3.

That sure was an eerie trip back into Pearl on the 10th. Ships still smoldering, bodies being ferried to the recreation landing, where there were stacks of coffins. That day, a seaplane took off and crashed over near Pearl City and the whole harbor got excited. Guess they thought it was another attack. After seeing the debacle of Pearl Harbor, I wondered if we had a Navy left to fight with. Truly though, I didn't worry about the big picture. I was perfectly happy to get to wherever we were sent.

By Paul V. Burchell

The morning of December 7, 1941, I was up on the main deck eating an apple when the planes started bombing. My first impression was that "the world was coming to an end."

When they sounded general quarters, I went to my battle station which was a pointer on a 1.1 on the starboard side of the bridge. Ammunition (shells) were knee deep and I believe we shot down at least two planes.

By James H. Medlin

Pearl Harbor. In brief, I was in the showers preparing for liberty. Dressed in only skivvies (bottoms only, half dry), I headed for battle station while discussing mock battle with Jo Valient, who was a gunner striker of turret one—my battle station. I was the left

Chapter Five

shellman of turret one during the length of time aboard. I was soon to find out this was not an imitation. We raced to our stations. Later, we were to strip decks, awnings, boom on starboard side, gangways, etc., to get underway. Jo and I dodged strafing planes when we were standing by the front hawser, attempting to cast it loose from *Honolulu*. *San Francisco* was tied up alongside another deck to our right. Our starboard side was free. *Honolulu* was tied up to a dock and we were tied up to her. I recall much of the action of the day, having been assigned to a large gun that we could not use in port, and therefore being on topside until we were well out of the harbor.

I was very young. I felt for the ones who were being murdered and had the urge to wipe out the Japanese fleet, as I'm sure we all did. I was under the impression that *St. Louis* could take on the entire Japanese fleet with victory. At least this was the thought of many of us younger sailors.

By Anthony Perille

I read an article that hit me just right. Neither my wife, nor my children, ever heard me talk about the Pearl Harbor attack. Betty Wilbur wrote about teenagers. I had just turned eighteen. I was bowhook on the number two motor whaleboat.

Saturday, December 6, 1941, we made a trip that took us alongside Battleship Row. It was a beautiful day. It was the day after Field Day. Those ships glistened in their peacetime dress. It was a beautiful sight. I was in the Navy almost a year then. My homesickness was almost gone. I loved *that* Navy, as we went by those great ships. I just sat there and took it all in.

The next day, Sunday, December 7, 1941, we had boat duty. Reveille sounded. I dressed and went to my boat to turn to, wiping the dew from it until mess call, when I went to eat. During chow, they called away our boat. I snatched up a doughnut and an apple, ran to the boat and we shoved off. We made the accommodation ladder. Our orders were to take a working party to Merry Point Landing, to wait for them, and bring them back to the ship.

When we got to Merry Point Landing, I laid down on a bench. The engineer came over and said I was beginning to look like an old salt. He started to wrestle with me. While down, I saw a plane dive and drop something. I thought it was one of our planes dropping bean bags again. But I noticed they were a lot bigger. By the time I got the engineer's attention, things were busting up all around us. We stood up. The torpedo planes were coming in on Merry Point to make their run. The planes were so close to us that the pilot's faces were very clear.

I said: "They're Japs! See the 'sun' on the planes?" As I was pointing it out, the plane exploded. We were now alone on the dock. A plane came and started strafing. We just ran. I landed in an excavation hole. Another sailor jumped in after me. He said he was scared. So was I, but I didn't want to show it.

So I said: "You'd better get used to it. This means war."

I thought about those ships. Profanity came out of me which was new for me. I stood up and saw a sailor waving a gun on the steps of the Administration building. I thought they were going to pass out guns, but they were getting up rescue parties. I ran back to Merry Point Landing, and met the coxswain. He said: "Let's get back to ship." I told him that we needed the engineer, but we had no trouble finding him, and so we shoved off, the attack all around us.

I stood up on the seats, took the bow line, held it tight and rode it like a water ski. The water was churning up pretty good and I was pointing out the debris to the coxswain. The rudder hit something which knocked it loose. He grabbed hold of the rudder and worked it by hand. We made it to the port bow where there was a jacob's ladder, but we didn't tie up the boats. I was the last to leave the boat. When I hit *St. Louis* main deck, my buddy Strong was firing away on his 50-caliber machine gun. He saw me. I waved and told him: "Get one for me."

His expression changed. I turned. A Japanese plane had just released a bomb which couldn't have been more than 70 feet from us. It hit the edge of the dock next to *Honolulu* and exploded. I took off for my battle station which was a 1.1 gun starboard aft. I had to get past the twin 5" gun mount, starboard side. It was swinging back and forth madly. At times there was only about 4" between it and the bulkhead. I had to get by. It was like playing Russian roulette. I timed it right and got through and went to my gun. Someone handed

Chapter Five

me a helmet; by this time, the noise was getting to me. I ripped off my T-shirt to stuff my ears, but no success, so I dropped it. Then I got busy. So many things were going on. I saw *Oklahoma* roll over, watched men walk up the sides, some slipping into the water. I happened to be looking toward *Arizona* when she got hit and blew up like a gas tank. And I swear I saw men on *San Francisco* throwing potatoes at the planes. A Jap plane came in eye-level between us and *San Francisco* and turned its belly to us. I could see the bullets ripping into it. Then there was a lull in the battle, which was a relief.

Nobody talked. They just looked. I think it was then that I saw *Nevada* pulling out; I wished we would. We were like sitting ducks. Looking the harbor over, it looked to me like we were prime to be hit next. Then the attack resumed.

Dive bombers were coming in dead astern and high. I wondered how I was going to go; I hoped fast. They started their dive. We opened fire. Our fire was well-concentrated, but we opened up too soon. We weren't reaching them. They peeled off and hit Battleship Row again. I can't say if we had gotten any of these planes; there was much confusion. For one, *Honolulu* was firing a 3" gun right over our heads. We weren't too far from its muzzle.

At one point, they started yelling. I asked them if they got one; they pointed it out. We cheered like we were at a baseball game. I felt our ship move; we were getting underway. Over the loudspeakers came the word: "All idle hands strip ship." That's when the swabs, brooms, and holy stones were deep-sixed. That too raised a cheer.

When we reached the channel, there was *Nevada* beached and on fire. Men were running around trying to do their job. Some were putting out fires, while others were lowering stretchers over the side. Our guns were still firing while going down the channel. I saw bomb-bursts in our wake. We finally reached open water. I felt a spray, and wondered why, but I was too busy to give it much thought. The starboard 5" gun mount swung down, fired, and swung back up again. I was told later that they had gotten a submarine, and the spray was from some torpedoes that hit a reef. The torpedoes were meant for us.

We fired at some planes; they must have been stragglers. My ears wouldn't stop banging away. It sounded like the battle was still going strong. On the third day, I figured I would see the doctor if they wouldn't stop by morning. By the fourth morning, it had stopped. It sure was a relief. I feel like Betty. When I see that flag raised, I have to fight tears.

By Cmdr. Fred Asher, USN (Ret.)

She's the most vivid memory I have of the Pearl Harbor attack. Watching her come out of Pearl Harbor at full speed was the thrill of a lifetime.

U.S.S. St. Louis - coming out of hell!

Chapter Five

I was busy making an attack on an enemy submarine at the time. The captain of *St. Louis* signaled, "Form on me to seek out and destroy the enemy." I thought, "Wow!" A couple of ships were going to attack the whole Japanese fleet!

As I recall, I signaled *St. Louis* that I had a submarine under attack and that a torpedo was heading for *St. Louis*. Fortunately, the torpedo was a miss. I like to feel that I may have had a small role in diverting or disrupting the attack of the submarines. Earlier, I had made two attacks on another submarine. I think we sank it.

I never saw a ship pass by faster or maneuver more violently than *St. Louis* standing out to sea. I had to take station on her and she was now far away. I put on 33 knots to try to catch up. It took a long time.

Battleship USS Nevada Saw St. Louis "A Symbol"

"As the USS St. Louis stormed past the blood-soaked decks of the torn and dying *Nevada* which had been beached to permit the *St. Louis* passage out of Pearl Harbor during the December 7 attack, the crew of the battleship cheered...there was nothing else for Americans to cheer that day, not on the *Nevada* alone but on a dozen other men-o-war which didn't leave the harbor."

"We sort of grabbed on to *St. Louis* as a symbol," the former *Nevada* sailor continued. "If she makes it, America makes it—that was the way we figured it."

"She did, America is, and what a debt of thanks her country owes *St. Louis* just for the inspirational sight of a graceful gray lady steaming out of hell, a great ship winning where the rest of the United States Pacific Fleet had lost."

First USN World War II Attack Group

The first U.S. Navy attack group of World War II was formed shortly after 1000 Honolulu time, Sunday, December 7, 1941.

It was formed to locate and attack an enemy carrier erroneously reported operating south of Pearl Harbor. *St. Louis* got underway for the avowed purpose for which it was built, manned, and trained—to seek out and destroy the enemy.

This first attack group consisted of the destroyers USS Montgomery (DM17), USS Phelps (DD360), USS Lamson (DD367), USS Blue (DD387), and the cruiser *St. Louis*, the only major warship to get underway and reach the open sea during the Japanese attack on Pearl Harbor.

The group was formed on signal from the senior officer present at sea in the Pearl Harbor vicinity. He was Capt. George A. Rood, USN Commanding Officer of USS St. Louis (CL49).

Sailors on the other ships said the "Fighting Lou" was just lucky, and loyal to their own ships, dubbed her the "Lucky Lou."

Chapter Five

DON'T GIVE INFORMATION TO STRANGERS.   At Sea.

<u>Orders of the Day</u>

Monday, December 8, 1941

0515	Reveille.
0530	Sound "General Quarters."
	When conditions warrant, and when ordered, set Condition Two.
0730	Breakfast.
0800	Muster on stations and make reports promptly thereof to the Executive Officer's office.

When time and conditions permit, strike anchor chain below to chain locker. Stow manila hawsers below decks. Stow Franklin buoys below.

Do such cleaning about ship as may be accomplished to keep things shipshape.

Notes: (1) Security officer- Lt. Cmdr. Townsend.
       (2) Working division- 2nd.
       (3) Each man is responsible for the care of his own gas mask and suit of protective clothing. He will have them at his battle station; when men are off watch, the masks will be slung to bunks or stowed in clothing lockers, and the protective clothing will be stowed in clothing lockers.
       (4) Use fresh water sparingly.

C.K. Fink
Commander, U.S. Navy,
Executive Officer

Chapter Six

The War-Time Patrols of the Lucky Lou: Part 1

A chronology of the Lucky Lou and World War II as compiled by D.J. (Doug) Huggins.

<u>1941</u>

December 10   Moored at Pearl Harbor, T.H.
December 12   Underway with USS Phoenix. Submarines fired torpedoes again, all missing. Destroyer escorts got two subs in the channel.
December 14   Sighted two periscopes.
December 16   Anchored in San Francisco Harbor.
December 16   Underway with convoy of ships. Three transports (U.S. Forces) and the Matson Liners. *Lurline*, *Matsonia*, *Monterey*, and two destroyers *Smith* (378) and *Preston* (379). More submarines.
December 21   Moored in Pearl Harbor, T.H.

* * * * * * * * * *

Declassified   December 25, 1941

From: The Commanding Officer
To: The Commander in Chief, U.S. Pacific Fleet

Chapter Six

Subject: Offensive Measures Taken During Air Raid, December 7, 1941—Report of

Reference: (a) Cincpac dispatch 102102 of December 1941

1. On December 7, 1941, this vessel was moored outboard of the USS Honolulu at Berth B-17, Navy Yard, Pearl Harbor, T.H.
2. At 0756 two of the ship's officers observed a large number of dark colored planes heading towards Ford Island from the general direction of Aiea. They dropped bombs and made strafing attacks. At the same time a dark olive drab colored plane bearing the aviation insignia of Japan passed close astern and dropped a torpedo. The air attack continued as is now known.
3. The ship went to general quarters at once and manned its entire battery.
4. The Commanding Officer reached the bridge at approximately 0800 and the ship's .50 caliber M.G. and its 1.1 battery was already manned and in action delivering a full volume of fire at the attackers.
5. Orders were given at once to raise steam in six boilers (two were undergoing routine cleaning) and to make all preparations for getting underway at the earliest possible moment. The reassembly of the two boilers being cleaned was commenced and they were on the line at 0400 on December 8th.
6. Yard work was in progress in all 5" mounts. Immediately all interferences were cleared away and the 5" battery was soon in operation, taking under fire the high-altitude bombers as primary targets and such other planes as presented themselves as secondary targets.
7. At 0931 the ship got underway, with boiler power for 29 knots, and stood out to sea via South Channel.
8. At 1004 when just inside the channel entrance buoys (buoys #1 and #2), two torpedoes were seen approaching the ship from starboard from a range of between 1,000 to 2,000 yards. Just before striking the ship, they hit the reef westward of the dredged channel and exploded, doing no damage to the ship.
9. At the source of the torpedo tracks, a dark gray object about

18" long was seen projecting above the water about 8". At the time, it was not positively known that this was part of a "baby" submarine but the Commanding Officer has since seen the one on display at the submarine base and is positive that the object sighted was the top of the periscope fairwater of a "baby" submarine.
10. The object was taken under fire by the starboard 5" battery from 1004 till 1007 but the ship is uncertain as to whether or not any hits were scored, although it was reported that hits were made on the first two salvos. The submarines very shortly (30 seconds approximately) disappeared from view.
11. The ship was proceeding at about twenty knots at this time and experienced difficulty in dodging the submarine, keeping off the reef, and in avoiding two mine sweepers and their sweep. However, it managed to clear and stood on out to sea at twenty-five knots and zigzagging.
12. An enemy carrier was reported to be operating to the south of Pearl Harbor and this vessel proceeded southward with the intention of locating and attacking the carrier.
13. For this purpose the commanding officer ordered the *Montgomery*, *Phelps*, *Lamson*, and *Blue* (then in the vicinity) to join us as attack group to engage the carrier. All vessels complied promptly and efficiently.
14. During this period enemy planes were fired on as follows:
    1016 – 1018: Four high-altitude bombers.
    1115 – 1117: Five high-altitude bombers.
    1145 – 1147: Three aircraft.
    No planes were seen to be shot down or damaged. The ship was not observed to be attacked by these planes.
15. At about 1100 the *Montgomery* signaled it had been ordered to make a magnetic sweep of the channel, and therefore, it was detached and ordered to carry out the orders for the sweep.
16. At 1134 a dispatch was received stating that an enemy vessel escorted by four others was south of Barbers Point heading east. The position given was due west of this vessel. Consequently course was changed to 270 degrees true in order to intercept.
17. At 1210 a despatch was received directing this vessel to attack

Chapter Six

an enemy ship reported as being five miles south of Barbers Point. Course was therefore altered to 357 degrees true.

18. At 1235 exchanged visual calls with the *Minneapolis* accompanied by two destroyers bearing 300 degrees true, range about 20,000 yards, standing to the northeastward.
19. At 1252 a despatch was received for this vessel to join the task force of Comdesbatfor (Detroit) and course was changed to 340 degrees true, that force being just then sighted bearing 345 true, distant about 25,000 yards.
20. During this phase enemy planes were fired on as follows:
    1213 – 1215: Group of four torpedo planes.
    1218 – 1222: Group of dive bombers.
    1233 – 1234: Group of planes (type not determined).
    All of the above firings were at long ranges. It is not believed that any damage was done. The ship was not attacked by these planes.
21. Thereafter the vessel operated as a unit of the force commanded by Comdesbatfor until its return to Pearl Harbor on December 10, 1941.
22. <u>Damage sustained</u>- some inconsequential machine gun bullet hits on upper decks and works; the only one of any importance being a hit that severed some of the strands of the port catapult cable.
23. Casualties to personnel – none..
24. <u>Damage inflicted</u>- It is felt that only in the rarest cases can any one ship positively state that it destroyed any specific plane or planes. However, bearing this in mind, the following planes are believed to have been shot down by this ship.
    (a) At about 1810 a large, single engine, dark olive drab-colored plane bearing the red ball insignia on each wing and with retracted landing gear was seen approaching at a low altitude (about 200 feet) from the direction of Barber's Point on a bearing of about 315 degrees relative. The plane was immediately taken under fire by the two .50 caliber and the one 1.1 machine guns on the port side forward. The plane altered course to the left until it was about paralleling the face of the dock and very nearly abreast the face of the dock

but still on the land side of it. The range was then about 300 yards. The first was then taken up by the corresponding guns on the starboard side. The plane climbed slightly and banked to the left, seemed to flutter a moment, then burst into flames and crashed being lost to sight behind buildings in the Navy Yard and in the prevailing smoke.

(b) At about 0830 a torpedo plane approaching from the direction of Merry Point and headed for the battleship was taken under fire by the after four .50 caliber and the 1.1 machine guns. It was flying at an altitude of about 50 to 100 feet. When just clear of the stern of the ship, the plane's engine was seen to fall out, the plane seemed to disintegrate and crashed in about mid channel and 150 feet past the ship. Its torpedo had not been released.

(c) At about 0900 a formation of six dive bombers was seen to be diving on the *Honolulu* and *St. Louis* from an altitude of about 6,000 to 7,000 feet on a relative bearing of 300 degrees. The dive was shallow (40 to 50 degrees) and the diving speed seemed slow (about 300 m.p.h.). The planes were taken under fire by the forward .50 caliber and 1.1" machine guns. Four of the planes sheered off to the left and released their bombs that landed in the water between 1010 Dock and Ford Island. All are believed to have exploded. The fifth plane was diving for this vessel and released its bomb which struck the water and exploded about 200 feet bearing about 5 degrees relative from the ship and exploded. The plane banked left caught fire and crashed. (It is believed that the sixth plane of this group dropped the bomb that damaged the *Honolulu*).

25. <u>Conduct of Personnel</u> – The Commanding Officer has nothing but the highest praise to give to each officer and man for their conduct, devotion to duty, willingness and coolness under fire and during the following days of most exhausting operations. When general quarters was sounded all hands proceeded quickly and without confusion to their stations exactly as though it were a drill. Throughout the entire action the whole ship performed to a degree of perfection that exceeded my

Chapter Six

most optimistic anticipation. This fine enthusiasm and spirit continues undiminished.

26. Officers and men that were ashore promptly returned to the Navy Yard and those that could join before the ship put to sea. Others joined other units wherever they felt that their services would be of value.

27. Lieutenant Charles A. Curtze, U.S. Navy of the Construction member of the Staff of Commander Cruisers, Battle Force, being quartered on board, proceeded at once, when the alarm was given, to Central Station where he took charge until relieved by the First Lieutenant and Damage Control Officer on his arrival on board from the city.

Lieutenant Charles A. Curtze

28. Special mention is made of the following cases:
    (a) Lieutenant Commander J.E. Florence, U.S. Navy, Lieutenant Commander Paul Jackson, DE-V(G), U.S. Naval Reserve, and Lieutenant R.N.S. Clark, U.S. Navy, arrived at the Navy Yard to find the *St. Louis* underway. They took to ships motor boat and tried to overhaul the ship.

Being unsuccessful, they then boarded a passing motor torpedo boat. This boat was short handed and they manned its machine guns but no planes attacked them. Failing to gain the *St. Louis* they then boarded the *Phoenix,* that was passing at that time, and served at sea on board that ship until December 10th.

(b) The splendid response and aggressive spirit displayed by the Commanding Officers of the *Phelps, Lamson, Blue,* and *Montgomery* in at once joining this vessel in the organization of an attack group.

29. <u>Ammunition expended</u>:
 5/38" A.A.– 207 rounds
 1.1/75– 3,950 rounds
 .50 Cal. M.G.– 12,750 rounds

* * * * * * * * * *

Dec. 26 Underway with same convoy as before. Evacuees (dependents) bound for the states.

Dec. 31 Anchored in San Francisco Harbor. Had liberty—and what a New Year's Eve!

<u>1942</u>

Jan. 2   Underway for San Diego with same convoy as before (transports empty).
Jan. 3   Moored to North Island dock in San Diego.
Jan. 4   San Diego Bay.
Jan. 5   San Diego Bay. I got liberty. (What 'cha know?)
Jan. 6   Underway at 1500 for unknown destination with Task Force 17, consisting of *Yorktown, Louisville, St. Louis,* and four destroyers: *Sims* (409), *Russell* (414), *Hughes* (410), and *Walker* (416). The convoy consists of *Lurline, Matsonia, Monterey* (with Fleet Marina Force), *Kaskaskia* (tanker),

Chapter Six

Lassen (ammunition ship) and *Jupiter* (cargo ship).

Jan. 14 Entered domain of King Neptune at 1351, crossing equator at longitude 151 degrees.

Jan. 20 Arrived off Pago Pago, Samoa, and operated in Samoan area while auxiliaries went into the harbor.

Jan. 24 Underway with *Yorktown, Louisville, Sabine* (tanker), and five destroyers: *Sims, Russell, Hughes, Walker* and *Mahan* (364). On course 310 degrees. Going to attack Japs on Marshall and the Gilbert Islands.

Jan. 27 Crossed equator going north, longitude 160 degrees; left *Sabine* and *Mahan*.

Jan. 29 Crossed international date line. Left the other four destroyers and headed for Marshall Islands at 25 knots.

Jan. 30 Steamed all day in that direction at 25 knots..

Jan. 31 At 0445 the *Yorktown* commenced launching planes. We were very few miles from the islands. At 0450 we came about on an opposite course still steaming at 25 knots. The planes returned to *Yorktown* at about 0600, loaded up and took off again. They returned this time about 0900. Very few planes were lost. During the afternoon a Japanese patrol bomber came over us. It dropped its bombs but they exploded a long way from us. *Yorktown* planes made duck soup of it in less than two minutes.

Feb. 1 Met *Sabine* and *Mahan*.

Feb. 6 Moored in Pearl Harbor at 1203. The other Task Force is in. The *Chester* received slight bomb hit. The *Enterprise* was flag ship of the other Task Force under Vice-Admiral W.J. Halsey. Rear Admiral Fletcher on *Yorktown* was command of ours.

Feb. 7 Received all Christmas packages and letters.

Chapter Seven

The War-Time Patrols of the Lucky Lou: Part 1

Accounts compiled
by D.J. (Doug) Huggins and Capt. R Semmes, (Ret.), USN.

<u>1942</u>.

Feb. 9   Moved into Pearl Harbor Navy Yard.
Feb. 18   Underway for States at 0900. Screened by two destroyers until we passed Molokai Island, then proceeded alone at 20 knots. We have aboard forty-five bags of mail, four captains, and about thirty men for transfer.
Feb. 23   Anchored in San Francisco Bay at 1050. Underway at 1300 for Mare Island Navy Yard.
Feb. 24   Moved into dry dock.
Feb. 28   Last day in dry dock.
Mar. 6   Moved out of Mare Island Navy Yard at 1200. Docked in San Francisco at 1430.
Mar. 10   Underway at 1430.
Mar. 11   Met Matson line *Lurline* and British liner *Aquitania* in the night on base course of 275 degrees at 20 knots.
Mar. 15   *Lurline* and destroyer went to Hilo, Hawaii.
Mar. 16   Arrived in Pearl Harbor.
Mar. 19   Underway to fire main battery practice. Have passengers and mail aboard. Met *Lurline* and *Aquitania* about 2000.

Chapter Seven

Mar. 24   Arrived safely in San Francisco Harbor. Docked at Pier 17.

Apr. 1   Underway at 1730 for Mare Island Navy Yard. Ran aground outside of yard channel because of thick fog. Underway again in about one hour.

Apr. 9   Underway at 1000 for San Francisco. At 1200 moored to Pier 48.

Apr. 11   Moved out of berth into channel.

Apr. 12   Underway at 1200 to fire 6" and 5" practice. A successful firing. At 1600 we met four freighters and one tin can. We have personnel of Patrol Wing Eight and Army mail aboard.

Apr. 14   Birth of the *Hubble Bubble*: Just before 8 o'clock reports, the gunnery officer, then LCDR J.R. McCormick, walked into the gunnery office and said to Al Seton: "I just had dinner with the captain. He wants a ship's newspaper. He's worried about morale. I've appointed you editor." "When do you want the first issue?" "Tomorrow morning. I've got the name of the paper for you. The *Hubble Bubble*. Just opened a dictionary and found it. Means a lot of noise. I have to make the 8 o'clock reports now."

Apr. 15   Today at about 1000 we passed a large convoy of twenty-four tankers, freighters, and cargo ships. Only two destroyers were escorting.

Apr. 23   Met USS Honolulu off the Christmas Islands with a six ship convoy and four destroyers. We left our ships ("President Tyler," "Kit Carson," "Benjamin Franklin," and "John Paul Jones") with *Honolulu*. We then headed south with a destroyer, USS Mugford (389). Crossed equator at 2130 on longitude 153 degrees.

Apr. 24   Steaming on course 180 degrees, at 16 knots, accompanied by *Mugford*. An enemy aircraft carrier reported to be in our vicinity.

Apr. 25   At about 1900 the radar picked up a target. We went to G.Q. and went over to the ship. It was *John Fremont* loaded with refugees, bound for San Francisco.

Apr. 26   Arrived at the French-owned island of Bora Bora, moored

The Saga of the Lucky Lou

Apr. 27
: alongside *Ramapo*, a small Navy tanker. Our passengers and mail for *Bobcat* have left the ship.
Moved out in the middle of the lagoon and anchored. All hands went overboard for swim. Beautiful water.

Apr. 29
: Underway from Bora Bora at 0700. At 1230 met USS Richmond with the liner, "President Coolidge." The *Richmond* turned back. Coolidge had refugees. We had soldiers from Bora Bora, and President Quezon of Philippine government.

May 1
: Steaming at 18 and 20 knots on course 020 degrees. Crossed equator this afternoon.

May 9
: Arrived at San Francisco at about 0900. Docked at Pier 42.

May 10
: Underway at 1100. At about 1300 we picked up our convoy of thirteen ships and two destroyers.

May 11
: On course 200 degrees to 240 degrees; speed 12 knots. Two more ships and one destroyer have joined us. The old tin can has left. Ships in the convoy:

USS Jarvis (DD393)
USS Henderson (AP1)
USS Lassen (AE3)
SS Talamanca (AF15)
SS Hercules (AK41)
SS President Grant
SS Moracstar
SS President Polk (AP103)
USS J. Franklin Bell (APA16)

USS Patterson (DD392)
USS Kitty Hawk (AKV1)
SS Playgos
USS Aldebaran (AF10)
SS Etolin
SS Alcoa Pennant (AK50)
SSHF Alexander
SS Antigua (AF17)

<u>Midway Girds for Battle</u>

For a long time, all U.S. military planners recognized the vulnerable position of Midway Atoll.

Shortly after March 10, 1942, when a Japanese four-engine "Mavis" was shot down forty-five miles west of Midway, Admiral Nimitz reached a considered opinion that a Japanese attack would strike Midway. By this time also, the Japanese code had been broken.

Based on these fragments pieced together, Nimitz's decision in

Chapter Seven

May 1942 was to wager nearly every warship in the Pacific Fleet to a position 300 miles northeast of Midway from which the Japanese could be intercepted. All he could scrape together were seventy-six ships.

The Japanese were sending 162 warships and auxiliaries, not counting small patrol craft and miscellaneous vessels.

The Japanese objective was threefold: invade and occupy strategic points in the western Aleutians and Midway as anchors in a new "ribbon" defense, with Midway as a base for raids on Pearl Harbor, and to draw out, and then annihilate, the U.S. Pacific Fleet in its hour of greatest weakness, before new construction could replace the losses at Pearl Harbor.

The most acute question before Admiral Nimitz's staff was whether to concentrate his attack on Midway, leaving the Aleutians to their fate, or to do something to protect the Aleutians.

After much discussion, on May 14, 1942, it was decided to form the North Pacific Force with the heavy cruisers USS Indianapolis (CA35), and USS Louisville (CA28), the light cruisers USS Honolulu (CL48), USS Nashville (CL43), *St. Louis*, and ten destroyers.

May 17 Arrived in Pearl Harbor. The convoy went into Honolulu.
May 18 Had a forty-five minute air raid alarm at about 1300 today.
May 19 USS Medusa moved alongside.

* * * * * * * * * * *

A Message from the Captain

To the Ship's Company: May 19, 1942

Three years in commission and a fine record the ship has made.

A ship is just so much machinery and it runs well or poorly depending on the skill of those operating it. It does not operate well unless every individual piece of machinery is ready to do its work properly and at the instant that it is needed. This, in turn, means that every person on board has a job to do and to do properly; he has the responsibility for his part that fits in the building of a smooth working whole that is the ship.

That this has been successfully done on *St. Louis* is proven by the record she has made and to each individual belongs his own and personal credit.

But more than being a lot of machinery, a ship has another something that is called the soul of the ship. That is the thing that makes good shipmates, makes the ship have get-up-and-go, makes her do her job a little bit better than the other fellow, and makes her a fast puncher and a hard hitter. *St. Louis* has this too.

The ship wouldn't be this way today unless those who put her in commission had not known their jobs and worked long and hard to give her the start that she got. We owe them much and to those who are still on board and to those who have been transferred, we want to express our appreciation of the solid foundation they built.

Since December 7th, we have had hard assignments and all hands can be proud of the fact that we have successfully completed every one of them, and, in addition, gotten quite a few "well done's" in the doing. We couldn't have done it unless we were all pulling together for the good of the ship.

We have a big responsibility to our country now, and as your captain, who has seen you change (in less than two minutes by the clock) from a peaceful and quiet Sunday morning to an all-guns-going war, I am sure that we will discharge that responsibility, and, in addition, uphold those fine traditions of our service.

It is a fine thing for any captain to know that his ship's company are steady, tried, and true, and that they can give it and take it. I have that feeling.

The Captain.

A Message from the Commander

The anniversary of *St. Louis* is also an anniversary of my arrival on board one year ago.

Many things have happened during that year, and many changes have taken place, but I must say that the crew has shown with each happening or change that they can do their stuff and do it well.

Chapter Seven

I am proud to be the Executive Officer of such a fine ship and excellent crew, and I wish all hands success in every endeavor which may be undertaken by our ship.

The Commander.

Dedication to Our Captain and Our Commander

We, the staff, have dedicated this edition to the task of publicly voicing the loyalty, appreciation, admiration, and esteem of the crew for the courage and brilliant leadership two great Americans have shown us this past year.

Not one of us know any other two men who are so highly regarded by all of those who come in contact with them. Our association this past year is something beautiful in the lives of fighting men and we thank God that we were chosen to serve under your command.

Captain Rood and Commander Fink, you lead; we will follow- anywhere!

Your Crew.

* * * * * * * * * *

May 22   Received an Admiral and his staff along with 200 tough Marines. Each is equipped with knife, pistol, etc. Others have rifles, tommy-guns, and Browning automatics.

May 23   Underway from Pearl Harbor at 0500. Steaming at flank speed of twenty-three knots on a northwesterly course, accompanied by USS Case (370). Literally armed to the teeth, "C" and "D" companies of the famed Second Marine Raider Battalion line the main deck of *St. Louis* from foremast to aft of turret five as the ship departs Pearl Harbor. Destination: Midway. Mission: <u>A last ditch stand on Midway by the Raiders if the Japanese attack, expected in five days, is successful.</u>

Their arrival on Midway is described by Walter Lord in his book *Incredible Victory*. He was still at it when some trucks roared up, throwing sand in all directions. A gang of men piled out, howling slogans and singing Chinese communist songs. Carlson's Raiders had arrived. This outfit—officially known as the 2nd Raider Battalion—was something of an experiment. Organized by Major Evans F. Carlson, its training reflected many ideas he had picked up with the communist forces in North China. It had the White House blessing, but its gung-ho philosophy smacked of indiscipline to too many old Marines. To say the least, Carlson's Raiders were controversial, but there was no doubt about their fighting qualities, and when Midway's hour came, Nimitz hurried out two companies. Arriving on *St. Louis*, along with Captain Miller's guns, "D" company went off to Eastern Island, while "C" joined Miller in the Sand Island woods. Both were a wild-looking lot. Bandoleers of cartridges hung from bronzed shoulders. Their pockets bulged with grenades. Their belts bristled with knives which they flung at the trees with casual skill. Even the medics were armed—no stenciled red crosses for this bunch.

By May 1942, the crew of *St. Louis* had settled down to a new routine: long patrols of wartime steaming with condition watches, general quarters, air defense calls, little or no liberty, infrequent mail deliveries, and ship's work and routine to be carried out.

The mess decks at meal times became the meeting ground for sailors who had made liberties together. These groups more or less sat regularly at the same tables. The mood was punctuated with gusty humor.

For the first two days the Marine Raiders were aboard, one of the young Raiders—a Corporal—regularly joined one of the tables of young petty officers from several divisions. The Marine always ate in silence. Quietly, the sailors would pass all the salt, pepper, sugar, canned milk and whatever condiments were on the table in front of him. When he finished his meal, always ahead of the sailors, he would be urged to go for "seconds" even though the crew was still lined up for "firsts." Always, he declined.

Just before arriving at Midway, right smack in the middle of a meal, the ship went to general quarters. "Airplanes?" someone

Chapter Seven

asked. "No, we would go to air defense," someone reminded him. "Must be the Jap fleet ahead of schedule," someone suggested as everyone scrambled for their battle stations. A ship paired against a fleet.

A few minutes later, the ship was secured from general quarters and everyone returned to the table. The Marine Raider was already there. He sat in silence while those at the table finished their meal. The corporal, tray in hand, stood up and said:

> I want to tell you men something. We Raiders have been watching your every move since we came on board. Just now, while you were at general quarters, we sat here, below decks, scared as hell not knowing what was going on and no place to dig in. We voted to tell you this and I'm the one elected to make this speech.
>
> When they told us we were coming aboard *St. Louis*, they told us we were lucky because we would be aboard the best and "most fightingest" ship in the Navy. They told us a little about you people and how lucky we would be to be with you. We thought that was just a lot of crap like a lot of things they have been telling us. So we watched you from the moment we came on board.
>
> While you were at general quarters, we discussed how you treated us. Gave us everything we wanted, let us ahead of you in the mess lines, let us have seconds before you had your firsts. Every one of us resented that, and we want you to know. We decided that we should not have taken advantage of that. We should have been the one who treated you like you treated us.
>
> We want you to tell your shipmates that we all have agreed that *St. Louis* is the best ship in the Navy. We hope we never see the Japs on Midway. Not because we are afraid of meeting them in hand-to-hand combat, in a last ditch stand that will be our job. We're the best there is at that, but we know that if the Japs ever land on Midway, it will only be because *St. Louis* is sunk and all of you are dead. We want you alive.

"C" and "D" companies of the 2nd Marine Raider Battalion never returned from World War II.

May 25 Arrived at Midway Island at 0900. The Marine Raiders and PBY personnel have been transferred. At 1900 underway from Midway harbor with the CASE. New course and speed- about 000 degrees true at eighteen knots. A large enemy task force is reported to be in the Northern waters.

May 28 Steaming northeast at seventeen knots.

May 31 Entered anchorage at Kodiak, Alaska, at 1200. At about 1600 the USS Sabine moved alongside and refueled us. We transferred flag personnel. At 1800 we were underway alone. Our mission or destination is unknown so far. Course is southeast at fifteen knots.

June 1 We are scouting now for the enemy force. Sea is very rough. Weather is cold and rainy.

June 2 We are continuing our search and have been joined by USS Nashville together with two old destroyers and the tanker *Sabine*. At 1730 a friendly S-type submarine broke surface at 12,000 yards. We are now in condition of readiness II when in bad weather.

June 3 Still searching for the enemy fleet. The USS Indianapolis, USS Louisville, USS Honolulu, and two destroyers. One is the USS Gridley (DD380), and other the USS McCall (DD400).

June 4 Force is continuing the patrol of the sea around Kodiak. We are refueling one by one from *Sabine*. Dutch Harbor and Midway Island were attacked today.

Chapter Eight

On our way north from Midway Island, I had a conference with Captain Rood about flight operation in the inhospitable North Pacific. He agreed to reduce our search missions to not more than 125 miles from the ship, compared with the 200 miles we had flown routinely in the South Pacific. This and Captain Rood's generally excellent knowledge of our capabilities and limitations did much to make successful flight operations possible. Even so, much of our five months in the Aleutians was frustrated by bad weather.

On June 3, 1942, Dutch Harbor was attacked by Japanese carrier-based planes, and the Battle of Midway raged in the period of June 4-6. *St. Louis*, with the cruisers *Nashville*, *Indianapolis*, and *Louisville*, plus four destroyers, had the mission of protecting the Aleutians from the attacking Japanese. We steamed around in the Aleutian fog, fearing collision with each other almost as much as with the enemy. On the 9th of June, *Honolulu* lost two planes and crews in very bad weather. With radio silence and no navaids, very accurate navigation was needed to find the ships after a search run with visibility frequently as low as a couple of miles, and sometimes much less.

In July, the task group made several unsuccessful runs against Kiska where the Japanese had landed and were establishing a base. The weather was so thick we never saw land, and the enemy probably never knew we were there. Admiral Theobald, our group commander, decided to return to Kodiak and regroup, and remarkably the sun came out and we were blessed with beautiful crisp days. We in the aviation unit used the interval to install the latest invention of Ray Moore, the unit's gunnery officer. He had discovered that the fixed firepower of our seaplanes could be doubled by installing an extra 30-caliber machine gun on the top wing. The "hold down" bolts of the gun just fit the holes in the wing designed for a camera gun installation. By running a lanyard from the gun to the cockpit, the pilot could give a yank and start firing. Best of all, the bullet path cleared the arc of the propeller by a couple of inches. The result of firing them both together was startling. One gun let go with a fast and furious rat-tat-tat; the other seemingly much slower and more sedate.

The effect on our morale of putting the extra gun on our old seaplanes was immediate and favorable. It gave us just the lift we needed to get out of the doldrums and on with the war. We felt sure we could fix those Kiska Japs now, in spite of the weather and the "zero" fighters on floats which the reconnaissance pilots had told us the Japs had now. We decided to keep our Moore machine gun installation to ourselves. The Bureau of Aeronautics might not look favorable upon our modification.

We were planning another Kiska run and this one had to work. Admiral Theobald's staff called in the aviators for a special briefing on our part in the new operation. Each cruiser (there would be a total of five) would launch two planes to act as spotting planes for the bombardment of the Jap base. Upon the completion of the bombardment, we would be recovered if conditions permitted. Otherwise we would be directed to fly to Dutch Harbor (600 nautical miles) and since this would be beyond our range after flying a spotting hop, the plans called for a small seaplane tender to hide in the island group halfway to Dutch Harbor to refuel us. It was hoped that this extreme would not be necessary. There would be no friendly fighter air cover for the operation because Kiska was far beyond the tactical radius of the Alaskan based army fighters, and no U.S. Navy aircraft carrier could be spared from the operation just now beginning in the Solomons.

The short time remaining before the bombardment passed swiftly. Early on the morning of August 7, 1942, the force was south of Kiska and ready for the run-in. The exact time of the action had not been set, but would most likely be determined by the weather.

Chapter Eight

The weather seemed to play the leading part in whatever went on in this strange land. As if to emphasize its importance, we ran smack into a thick fog bank when thirty miles from Kiska, but Admiral Theobald was not to be denied this time.

We steamed onward, passes alternately through clear spaces and fog banks. We wondered if our previous abortive attempts in this area had alerted the Japs, and if they would be lying in wait for us. They had plenty of surface ships to spare, some for Kiska support, although the Battle of Midway had hurt them badly in carriers when they had lost four. They were known to have a powerful undamaged battleship force, whereas our own had been badly mauled at Pearl Harbor and was not now a factor in the Pacific War. Submarines were a constant worry and were always in our thoughts. Several enemy subs had been sighted in Aleutian waters and we felt sure there were some around now. As far as we knew, the Japs had not yet succeeded in building a land air base on Kiska or any other nearby island. We did expect some air opposition in the form of seaplane bombers and "zero" fighters on floats.

St. Louis aviation unit remained at flight quarters most of the day of the run-in. Periodically, the planes would be warmed up so they would be ready to go on short notice. Ray Moore was the pilot to go in the second plane and we were beginning to get a little nervous with anticipation. Finally, word came down from the bridge talker that we were really going in, and the planes would be launched in about fifteen minutes. The indecision was over and the weather seemed not so nasty now. I told Chief Pepin to top off the planes with gas since they had been turned up many times and had probably used several gallons apiece in the process. It must have been a premonition of need—I had never felt it necessary to top off the tanks before if they had been run down a bit—but now it seemed very important.

Ray and I climbed into our planes and got ready for the catapulting. My radio-gunner was Norman, and Gibb was going with Ray. We were launched at 1745 local time. The other cruisers also catapulted their aircraft, and within five minutes the ships had disappeared from sight in another fog bank. Ray and I climbed to 2000 feet, which was just above the cloud layer. Two planes from the cruiser *Honolulu* joined up with me and we flew around in formation waiting for the ships to run into a clear area. We couldn't see anything over the sea or land. Finally, I decided to head north and see if I could make landfall. We broke out of the overcast over Kiska near Vega Point. It was a strange feeling, to see at last this Jap-held territory after our struggle to beat the weather to get here. I proceeded back to the ship and found her now passing through alternate layers of fog and clear. I passed the bearing of the harbor to the ship and we remained circling in her vicinity till she cleared the fog bank about ten miles off the Kiska South Coast. I led my plane section to an area where there was some chance of spotting. *Honolulu's* planes broke off and went about their own business. We could see the hill around Kiska Harbor all right and we had enough altitude, but the harbor itself looked like a mass of fog.

At 1940 our ships opened the bombardment. They were firing full salvos and we could hear the firing above the noise of our own engines. Ray and I flew over Little Kiska Island and climbed to get above the overcast. We were looking for a hole to spot through when we saw the leading destroyer shift fire to anti-aircraft bursts. We saw the plane she was firing at, and another one above us commenced a diving approach toward us. I was at 2000 feet and commenced a steep power spiral through the overcast, and leveled off at 200 feet to find that the fighter had not followed. We were in the clear now and flew toward the destroyer group, but we could still see nothing in the harbor. Another fighter was sighted ahead, and as he came in he was taken under fire by a destroyer and then he turned away. During this time, all ships were firing on schedule and they would occasionally take an enemy plane under fire.

At 2010, the ships ceased firing and changed course. We flew to *St. Louis* and began to circle. Almost immediately she signaled to "proceed as previously directed," which meant for us to fly on up the chain to Dutch Harbor via the small seaplane tender stationed at Atka. We had hoped for recovery by the ship as we had already been in the air for the two and a half hours. Also, there was only about two hours of daylight left—not enough to reach Atka. There was nothing to do but get as far along our course as we could before nightfall, so we continued to climb until we broke out of the overcast at 3000

Chapter Eight

feet. We found later that the ships had feared a bombing attack at recovery time and Captain Rood did not think the ships would have a chance to slow to pick up their planes. He had sent us the signal to go ahead to give us a little head start. Actually, the bombers returned to base without attacking and the other cruisers did recover aircraft. Thus, Ray and I, and the radiomen, were alone now on our "Aleutian adventure" and Dutch Harbor was 600 nautical miles away.

The small island we had intended to take departure from was completely obscured, so we were in some doubt as to our position. We never did get a good point of departure, but took up the prearranged course of 084 degrees and hoped we were not far off at the start. About 2100, Sugar Loaf Head was identified and we knew we were pretty close to track, though somewhat to the south. We passed close to Tanaga Volcano and started to land off the coast, as there was a break in the overcast and we could see the island short. I took one look at that Tanaga coastline and it looked so rocky and uninviting that I decided to go on although it was already after sunset. We set course in general direction of the next island, Kanaga, found a hole, spiraled down, and landed about halfway between Tanaga and Kanaga. I cut my engine and prepared to wait out the night, which turned out to be one of the strangest I ever spent. Ray Moore had landed with me and now the two of us were riding the waves about 100 feet apart. I had arranged with Ray before landing that we would try for an 0700 takeoff the next morning.

The landing had been made at 2230, and in the beginning the weather began to clear with stars overhead. About midnight, a dense fog descended and the air got much colder. I lost contact with the other plane. The sea was not very rough, but there was a moderate swell which made the seaplane pitch a great deal. The excitement of the day and hour had combined to bring an aching tiredness to my body. Realizing that the real test of whether we could get back would occur on the next day's flight, I resolved to try and get some sleep. Have you ever been defeated by the perversity of an inanimate object? Well, I was that night. The object turned out to be the cockpit hatch cover. The lock, through long usage, had picked this moment to become sufficiently worn enough to just refuse to stay locked. I would close the cover to keep out the cold and leave my hand to hold the lock down. As soon as I dropped off to sleep, the cover would fly open again. I tried sleeping with the cover open, but the wind was too cold. Finally, toward dawn, I got the cover to stay locked by jamming a pencil in the mechanism.

Just after getting this solved, I was awakened from a fitful dozing by hearing surf breaking. All though of sleep banished, and I was suddenly awake, visions of being dashed on some inhospitable Aleutian rock racing through my head. I started the engine and taxied away from the noise of the surf till I could hear it no more. By the time I had another catnap, dawn was breaking in a discouraging sort of way. The fog was as thick as any I had ever seen. It clung to the surface of the water and completely engulfed our plane with its wet vapor. There was no sign of Ray through this heavy curtain, though he might have been near for all I know. At 0715, I heard his engine start, run for a while, and then roar into full power for takeoff. Ray was not far away—maybe 500 yards. I fired a star to make sure he didn't run me down, but I didn't see him at all, and soon I was left alone on a cold, fog-bound sea. I called Ray on my radio but heard nothing. I waited a few minutes to see if the fog might lift a little, but it only seemed to thicken. I ran over in my mind the choices open to me—there wasn't really much. I could stay where I was and wait for a weather improvement, but my previous Aleutian experience reminded me that it might take days or even weeks. I could take off in the fog and try to navigate somehow to Nazan Bay on Atka, where the seaplane tender rendezvous was supposed to be. Well, there was no point in giving in to the weather without a struggle.

At 0730, I started the engine, then taxied in circles till the engine was warm. When all was set for takeoff, the fog remained close to the water and so thick I had to make an instrument run to get airborne. As soon as we cleared the water, I put the old SOC in a gentle spiral climb to avoid smashing the mountains. At 4,000 feet we broke out on top, and the warm sunshine above the cloud layer was beautiful and so welcome that its effect on our spirits was like magic. I sighted the summit of Kanaga Island Mountain to the north, and from our relative position calculated that we had drifted almost due south during the night for fifteen miles in spite of a moderate west wind. We headed north to get on track and then took up course

Chapter Eight

084. There gradually appeared some breaks in the undercast which began to give me some navigational help. We passed over, and definitely identified, Kulak Bay on Adak Island. It was a great feeling of satisfaction to know exactly where I was for a change. We continued on to Atka over about nine-tenths cloud cover and found a hole just short of where I figured the island should be. I sighted land to starboard and continued parallel to it until land also appeared to port. It looked like a dead end, but as I got nearer I could make out a valley between the mountains and saw water on the other side. We flew through the valley at 50 feet altitude with a 150 foot ceiling and landed in a bay on the other side. At first I thought this was Nazan Bay, the rendezvous point, but there was no ship here. With the ceiling so low, I decided to wait for an improvement before trying to find the seaplane tender, so we anchored close to the shore at 0915. Norman and I were both tired after our almost sleepless night on the open sea. This bay was calm and we both fell asleep without difficulty, sleeping for some little time.

After awakening, I found that the ceiling had improved a little and it appeared that we might be able to scout around to fix our position, and with luck find our refueler. We took off and investigated the coast of the island very closely. I decided we were definitely on the SW coast of Atka, so I landed to make out a position report to send to *St. Louis* on the slim chance they might pick it up. While I was working on the report, I had Norman check our float gas tank. We were using it now as I had flown the other tanks dry. We carried a stick with which to sound this tank, and it showed that we now had 20 gallons left. We had taken off with 170 from the ship only yesterday. So much had happened that my shipboard life was beginning to fade into unreality—surely it was longer ago than yesterday.

We got airborne again and streamed the trailing wire antenna for our radio. Norman sent the message giving our position and I wondered, as I listened on my earphones to his expert rendition of the Morse dit-dah's, if anyone anywhere received it.

At 1430 came a break which changed the outcome of this flight. I sighted an old type destroyer about twelve miles off the coast and almost feared a mirage—it had been over sixteen hours since I had last glimpsed any human being (besides Norman in the rear seat).

The Saga of the Lucky Lou

The last had been Ray Moore as darkness had descended the night before. The ship was still there, so I figured it must be real and maybe it was our refueler. As we neared, I identified myself and had Norman send the flashing light: "Do you have gas?" The ship sent back, "Can you land?" We answered the question by acting it out. We landed and taxied to the fantail of the ship which had now stopped. It did indeed turn out to be our refueler, the USS Hurlbut, and a more beautiful sight I have never seen. She refueled us (we were now down to five gallons- enough for about twelve minutes of flying) and also send over by line hot coffee and sandwiches which were most welcome. The captain of the ship gave me the latest weather forecast which read fog all the way to Dutch Harbor, now about 300 miles away. He said if I was doubtful of making it, he would take Norman and me aboard and sink the plane. It was tempting, but after twenty-one hours in the plane, from the Japs at Kiska through the Aleutian fog to here, it was just not the way to end a flight. It was 1515 by the time I was ready to take off, with the plane so heavily loaded that I could barely get it flying in the calm sea. Regardless of what else happened on my attempted flight to Dutch Harbor, I should not have fuel trouble because we were now loaded to 170 gallons again...

After some difficulty getting airborne again with the heavy load in the smooth sea, we turned northwest to seek the Naval Station at Dutch Harbor.

It became apparent soon after leaving the Hurlbut that I would have to go above the overcast. Even though there were some areas of good visibility, there were others of practically none at all, and I [sic] had to fly as to avoid running into these islands whose mountains reached upward 7000 feet above the sea. I passed Sequam Island abeam while flying just above the overcast at 6000 feet, and almost an hour later passed the first of the Islands of Four Mountains. The overcast was high now with no holes anywhere. The flying had become very dreary and depressing as we were now between two solid dark gray layers. No sign of the earth below or the blue sky which must be above somewhere. I was carrying a 20 degree drift correction which I had gotten from an estimate from drift along the Four Mountain islands. This correction, which quite possibly was

Chapter Eight

off to some extent, could drift me over the islands or out to sea. I was sorely in need of a break to prove my navigation before trying a letdown through 6000 feet of fog. The layers we were flying between gradually seemed to merge. In looking ahead, or in any other direction, nothing could be made out in the gray same-ness of the clouds. There was no longer any cloud horizon to help me in keeping the plane level. I was strictly on instruments even though the plane was not actually in the clouds. Should I climb up on top, as I had after the night on water at Kanaga? The heavy thickness above might extend upward far beyond our ability to climb. Also, once in that grayness, I would have no warning if mountain peaks should be in our path. A descent through the fog carried the same danger of running into the land. It was better to keep this altitude where I at least had a little forward visibility to give warning of danger ahead.

Time seemed to drag interminably. I would glance at the clock on the instrument panel, then fly on for what seemed a great interval, only to find at next check that a mere three minutes or so had gone by.

When my log showed the Umnak Coastal Plan was due abeam by dead reckoning at 1755, there was still nothing but thick gray clouds to see. At last, after flying nearly an hour without seeing anything but clouds, there appeared a marvelous funnel shaped hole in them, going down steeply all the way to the ground. At the bottom of it, like some scene from an unlikely movie, was the Army base at Umnak Island. I was right on track after all! Before the funnel had a chance to dissipate, I dived through it so fast that I rattled the wings of the old SOC and pulled out at 500 feet over the glorious land. The rest of the way to Dutch Harbor was managed under the clouds by picking a careful way along the south coast. Norman and I were relaxing a bit for the first time we could remember. I had my fill of the mixture of fog and mountains and felt no desire to climb through that stuff again. I finally got out of the cockpit for the first time in twenty-six hours, including twelve and a half hours of flying. Ray Moore was at the dock to meet me and greeted me with, "Who do you think you are, Lindbergh?" I found out that he had found the refueler, then joined up with PBY patrol plane returning to Dutch Harbor, and flown wing on him back to base.

Ray and I waited several days before getting orders to rejoin *St. Louis* at Kodiak. We flew together up the chain the rest of the way without incident. It seemed somewhat mild after the first 600 miles over the uninhabited and deserted sea. I felt my Aleutian adventure drawing to a close...nearing the entrance to Kodiak Harbor, we sighted *St. Louis* down below, by a strange coincidence arriving at the same time as we. Flying nearer, we let them get a good look at us, close enough to read the side numbers.

Scout Observation Craft (SOC)

They recognized us all right. I could imagine Captain Rood up on the bridge seeing us for the first time since we had catapulted into our adventure a week before. The signal bridge began sending a message by blinker, which I knew came from Captain Rood. Norman and I read it together. It was simple, but complete and it got a wealth of meaning into just two words: "Welcome home."

When *St. Louis*, in company with the Yorktown and Enterprise groups, arrived at Pearl Harbor after the Marshall and Gilbert Islands raids, the harbor was in an unusual state of attention—literally, because ships in port had manned the rail to greet the returning units. It was as if, at last, there was a little something to take to the

Chapter Eight

heart over. The fleet had at last struck a blow at the enemy.

I would like to describe the excellent aviation facilities that the cruiser *St. Louis* and her sister ships had. As you will recall, all the battleships lacked any storage place for the aircraft other than the main deck and the catapults themselves. There was no protection from sea, or gun fire (either from the enemy or from your own ship). The first treaty cruisers of the Indianapolis class managed a considerable improvement by going to hangars on the main deck amidships, and elevated catapults requiring a long lift up by crane for any plane moved from either port or starboard hangar to be launched. The *St. Louis* class seemed to reach the ultimate of efficiency in hangar design to facilitate air operations. This was possible because the ship had a high freeboard aft, and a square stern giving an excellent storage space where all four planes could be taken below and covered over with a sliding hangar cover. During heavy weather or times when flight operations were not expected, the planes could be worked on in comfort below decks. The key to this was building into the airplane elevator, and hangar deck itself, a guiding track system for handling the small-wheeled carts in which the main pontoon of the SOC rested. If flight operations were expected, one plane would be hoisted aboard each catapult while the other two remained in the hangar with wings folded. After the launching of the first two aircraft, the others would be brought up in turn, the wings unfolded and they would be placed in position for launch. If all went very well, all four planes could be airborne in slightly over four minutes from receipt of the signal "launch aircraft."

Upon return from the flight operation—when four planes had been airborne—they would circle the ship until receipt of the recovery signal. In calm seas, a dog recovery could be made with the plane landing parallel to the ship's course, then taxiing onto the recovery net while being trailed from a trained out-catapult. The amidships crane would lift the plane aboard, and place it on the elevator for wing fold and moving below on its track cart. Succeeding planes would follow with two left on the catapults if subsequent flight operations were anticipated. The more usual recovery, the cast type, involved a ship's turn of 90 degrees through the wind line and was used when a choppy sea needed smoothing out to make a landing place. This slick gave a relatively good water for the plane to touch down while landing into the wind. As soon as the plane slowed, which was quickly in a seaplane, the pilot turned toward the trailing net and taxied aboard until he felt he was in position to cut his power. If he managed this successfully, the plane would drop back, but a spring-loaded hook on the bottom of the pontoon would catch into the webbing of the net and tow the plane along until it could be hooked on to the crane for hoisting aboard. Back and forth turns through the wind line by the ship would make additional slicks for the other planes to land in their turn. It was the job of the radioman gunner to stand over the pilot's cockpit and unrig the sling from its wing stowage, then effect a mating of it with the crane hook while the plane was bouncing on the net and the hook was swinging to and fro. A good juggling act was required when sea conditions were adverse. During this phase, the pilot held onto the radioman's legs to keep him from falling overboard. The hook-on was a critical step, but the hoisting could be a bit on the exciting side, particularly if the ship was rolling very much. To prevent the pontoon or wings from smashing into the fantail, the V-division aircraft handling crew would man long poles, with padded U-shaped ends, to steady the plane as it was being hoisted up the considerable distance from the sea to the deck of the St. Louis. Built-in small, flexible cables were also attached to lines from the ship during this hoisting phase. There were occasional mishaps, but the SOC's were ruggedly built and most damage was minor and could be repaired by the excellent mechanics and metalsmiths aboard.

 The catapulting of the St. Louis aircraft was accomplished through the use of the 5-inch powder charges rigged to accelerate the launching cart down the greased track. The catapult officers were instructed to launch the plane on an up-roll of that side of the ship. The aviators sometimes complained that for perversity they would launch on the down-roll instead. The launching itself was a sudden and violent affair. The airplane engine was revved to full power upon signal of the launching officer. The pilot locked the throttle quadrant tight, gave a "launch o.k." signal, and rested his head against a cushioned back rest. Shortly thereafter, there was a muffled boom and a rapid acceleration from zero to sixty knots in the sixty feet of catapult run. When the plane got to the end of the catapult, two hydraulic bumpers stopped the cart and the pontoon, airplane, pilot, radioman, and assorted equipment was now flying over the sea. Flaps were retracted as speed was gained and the mission was underway.

June 5	Our patrol and search is continued at 15 knots. *Nashville*, *Sabine*, and one old destroyer have gone in to Kodiak.
June 6	*Nashville* has returned. She has the flag. Cruising as before.
June 7	Our patrol is continued in the vicinity of Kodiak. No contact as yet.
June 8	*Nashville* and *Indianapolis* have gone to Kodiak.
June 9	*Nashville*, *Indianapolis*, *Gridley*, and *McCall* have returned with *Sabine*. We refueled this afternoon.
June 10	Patrol continued from 57 degrees latitude to as far south as 42 degrees.
June 11	*Honolulu* lost two planes today because of bad weather. We have found no trace of planes or crews as of yet.
June 12	Continued patrol in Alaskan area in bad weather.
June 13	Very dense fog today. Used radars to keep our position. At sundown, all ships except destroyers got in column and used a towing spar.
June 14	Weather a little improved. Refueled from *Sabine* at 0900.
June 15	At 0600, we were joined by eight more destroyers—three new, 5 old. Force now consists of two heavy cruisers, three light cruisers, one tanker and twelve destroyers.
June 17	*Indianapolis*, our flag ship now, has gone to Kodiak.
June 18	A destroyer and the tanker *Kaskaskia* have joined us.
June 19	Refueled today from *Sabine*. Also received a few stores and sent empty powder cases to her. Sent

	mail too. She left later.
June 22	Refueled from the *Kaskaskia*.
June 24	At 0800 was on 50 degrees latitude. Later headed south again.
June 25	*Indianapolis* has returned and *Honolulu* and one destroyer left. Steaming north today.
June 28	Refueled from *Kaskaskia* this morning. Operations continued as before between 56 degrees and 40 degrees latitude. Weather is always cold, varies from rainy to fair.
June 29	*Honolulu* has returned.
June 30	We left the force at 0600, headed for Kodiak at 18 knots accompanied by a destroyer.
July 2	Arrived at "Women's Bay" this morning. At 1300, *St. Louis* moved up the bay to the dock.
July 3	The supply ship *Artic* (F7) and a destroyer have moored alongside. *Kaskaskia* and a destroyer also came in shortly after.
July 4	Provisioning ship from *Artic*.
July 5	Underway to rejoin the force accompanied by *Brooks*.
July 6	Passed *Louisville* this morning. She is headed for Kodiak.
July 7	Joined our force about 1100. Received mail which is the first since our departure from Pearl Harbor. It was delivered to us by the tanker *Guadalupe* now of our force.
July 8	Refueled from *Guadalupe* today.
July 9	*Indianapolis*, *Nashville*, and three destroyers have left us.
July 12	*Louisville* has returned from Kodiak with a destroyer.
July 13	Met the *Kaskaskia* and *Aylwin* (355). Refueled from her. Also transferred mail and personnel.
July 14	*Honolulu* and *Kaskaskia* have left us.
July 15	Patrolling with *Louisville* and *Guadalupe* and two destroyers. Left them at 1900 and headed 328

Chapter Eight

	degrees at 15 knots.
July 16	Met *Nashville* and *Reid* (369).
July 18	Met *Honolulu, Guadalupe,* and a destroyer and four minesweepers this morning.
July 19	Met *Gridley* (380) this morning. We are headed for Kiska Island to bombard the Japs there.
July 20	Met *Indianapolis, Louisville,* and two destroyers. During the rendezvous, *Reid* dropped depth charges on a supposed sub. Refueled the minesweepers. *Guadalupe* turned back after we refueled and we headed southwest toward Kiska.
July 21	Refueled *McCall* (400) while the other cruisers each refueled a destroyer. Two PBY's came over about that time. At 1200 we went to general quarters to rehearse our plan of battle. We attack tomorrow afternoon. Task Force Eight is composed of two heavy cruisers, three light cruisers, five destroyers and four minesweepers. They are as follows:

Cruisers:
(35) *Indianapolis*- flagship.
(28) *Louisville*
(49) *St. Louis*
(43) *Nashville*
(48) *Honolulu*

Destroyers:
(400) *McCall*
(380) *Gridley*
(370) *Case*
(369) *Reid*
(354) *Monaghan*

Minesweepers: (4) (9) (12) (232)

July 22	Our attack has been called off until the weather is better. It was scheduled to be launched at 1700 but visibility is only about 500 yards. We are steaming at 10 knots not far from Kiska.
July 23	Bombardment again held up by heavy fog. We are headed east to refuel.
July 25	Refueled *Long* this morning. Met *Guadalupe*; heavy cruisers refueled.
July 26	All ships were refueled by 0800. We then left *Guadalupe* and are now steaming toward Kiska

	again at 20 knots. Attack tomorrow.
July 27	Refueled a minesweeper. Went to general quarters at 1300 and secured at 2200 without firing a shot. The fog was so thick three minesweepers collided. We advanced as far as thirty miles of the island but fog was too heavy.
July 28	Started in to attack again today but the fog was too heavy. The bombardment has been indefinitely postponed. We are now headed east at 20 knots.
July 29	Headed for Kodiak at 20 knots. The three damaged minesweepers have gone to Dutch Harbor.
July 31	Entered Kodiak Harbor or Women's Bay in column. *St. Louis* and *Louisville* moved alongside *Ramapo*, refueled, then anchored out. *Nashville*, *Honolulu*, and *Indianapolis* went to Air Station dock.
August 1	Moved up with *Louisville* to the dock.
August 3	Underway from Kodiak at 1830 with the task force. Headed south at 14 knots.
August 6	Met *Elliot*. Headed for Kiska again and the weather has been clear so far because winter is approaching the north. The Task Force rehearsed the bombardment plan this afternoon. We attack tomorrow if weather conditions are favorable. Refueled the destroyer *McCall* (400) this afternoon. Other cruisers are fueling small vessels also.
August 7	Today we bombarded the Jap occupied Island of Kiska- eight months after Pearl Harbor. We started our approach at 1645 on course 270 degrees. At 1750 all cruisers launched two planes each for spotting purposes. At 1755 the nearest land was 25,000 yards (radar range). We were on our firing course at 19,000 yards, but could not see a thing. So we finished the run and then came about for another attempt. By the time we were in range, land was sighted at 19,100. We advanced at 20 knots. When on the firing course at 19,000, we commenced firing. The time 1958 and 50 seconds. The

Chapter Eight

bombardment lasted until 2011. At 2015, we fired our first shells at aircraft directly overhead. The island was burning in several places by now. The aircraft continued the attack on us long after we had completed the bombardment. We are now steaming east at 25 knots, covered by darkness and thick fog. Ammunition expended today was: main battery- 1228 rounds. AA Batter- 440 rounds and a large quantity of machine gun ammunition. Total weight sixty tons. This morning we sank a floating mine. Our planes have headed to Atka, 250 miles east of Kiska.

August 11 — Moved into Women's Bay today. Moored alongside *Louisville* at 1430. All ships moored close by except *Honolulu*.

August 14 — *Indianapolis*, *Nashville*, and *Honolulu* moved out today.

August 15 — Not much to do up here. One can either go get soused or go to "Bell Flats" fishing. Fish (trout and salmon) are very plentiful up here. Also we pass many whales on our operations at sea. Plenty bluestone crabs too.

August 19 — Underway with *Louisville* and escorting destroyers. As we enter open sea we pass *Indianapolis*, *Nashville*, *Honolulu* and two destroyers coming in. They have been firing a gunnery practice.

August 22 — Fired AA target practice.

August 23 — Received small-pox inoculation shot.

August 24 — Arrived at Kodiak Harbor, anchored, moved alongside *Cuyuma* to refuel, then moored to a buoy.

August 25 — *Indianapolis*, *Louisville*, *Honolulu* and four destroyers put to sea.

August 26 — Underway with *Nashville*, four old destroyers—232, 242, 14, 235—and two fast troop transports, *J. Franklin Bell* and another. They are equipped with landing boats and gear as well as personnel for landing operations (in a few days).

The Saga of the Lucky Lou

August 28	Passed through Unimak Pass this morning. Passed into the Bering Sea and by Dutch Harbor. Another transport and more tin cans have joined us. Eight four-pipers so far for numbers of two (243) and (250).
August 29	Refueled two destroyers. Met a large convoy of small craft, 25-30 boats, this afternoon, consisting of destroyers, Canadian "Vorvettes", tugs, barges and cranes. Start operations of landing on Adak Island in the morning.
August 30	Started landing troops and equipment on Adak at 1400. We have met no opposition thus far. *Nashville, St. Louis,* and destroyers are now patrolling the waters around the island. It is immensely rough and cold. The two transports have gone, each into a different lagoon beyond the bay, together with PT boats and the rest of the small boats.
August 31	Still patrolling around Adak. Met *Indianapolis, Louisville, Honolulu,* and destroyers this afternoon.
September 2	Fueled *King* and then refueled from *Cuyama*.
September 3	Steaming east at 20 knots, all night and today, with *Honolulu* and two destroyers. Arrived off Dutch Harbor on the Island of Unalaska about sundown. Picked up one freighter.
September 4	Two more cargo ships have joined us. We are now steaming toward Adak. Met *Indianapolis, Louisville,* and *Nashville. Honolulu* left and *Nashville* took her place.
September 5	Arrived off Adak. Destroyer picked up a sub and dropped depth charges, results unknown. Cargo ships went in and we are headed back toward Dutch Harbor.
September 6	Met *Indianapolis, Louisville, Honolulu,* and destroyers. Are now patrolling waters of Bering Sea around Adak. Bring on that so-called rough North Atlantic.
September 9	*St. Louis* and two destroyers left the task force last

Chapter Eight

	night and we have been steaming east all day.
September 10	Passed through Unimak Pass last night. One destroyer has left.
September 11	*St. Louis* and *Kane* entered Kodiak Harbor through the small channel and moored at the Air Station dock at 1000. The ships all enter through the narrow channel because the old entrance is mined.
September 13	Underway with *Franklin Bell, Kane, Elliot,* and *Lawrence*. Headed for Adak. *Casco* (seaplane tender) was torpedoed off the Dutch Harbor coast about August 30. A PBY dropped depth bombs which caused the sub to surface. *Casco* went into port under its own power. *Kane* was sent to take off the crew and then destroy the sub.
September 14	Proceeded through Unimak Pass into the Bering Sea on the 8 to 12 watch. We always pass through at night because of enemy submarines.
September 15	The sea is very rough as well as the weather. The North Atlantic is nothing compared to this. Met *Honolulu*, a transport and destroyers just out of Dutch Harbor.
September 16	Sea still rough as before with rolls of 30 and 35 degrees now and then. *Bell* and destroyers have gone to Adka about fifty or a hundred miles east of Adak. At 1500 we were off Adak and the other transport went in. The beach was in sight for a short time.
September 17	Sent *Honolulu* plane to *Honolulu*. We recovered it for her about a week ago. We lost one of ours. The Army bombed Kiska again on the 15th and did much damage. I didn't know it, but we have sailed east to Unalaska Island again and have a transport now.
September 18	Now cruising west again for Adak. Fueled *King* and *Sand*. Passed *Indianapolis, Louisville, Nashville,* and four destroyers. *St. Louis, Honolulu,* the transport and two cans on course for Adak.
September 19	Left the transport at Adak after she liked to have

rammed us, caused by the wrong translation of signals on her part. We then met the rest of the force and refueled from *Cuyama*. Commander C. K. Fink, our executive officer, was put on the tanker. He came aboard with Captain Rood in Mare Island over a year ago. We all hated to see him go. *Honolulu* left for Mare Island, damn it.

September 20   A year ago today we were en route from Manilla to Honolulu. *Nashville* left us at sunset to go to Kodiak to change command.

September 30   *St. Louis* and *Nashville* are now proceeding toward the enemy supply route north of Attu. *St. Louis* is in command.

October 10   Saw Attu this morning and her snow-capped mountains. We have seen no trace of the enemy so far.

October 15   Passed into the North Pacific by way of the strait between Kiska and Attu.

October 18   Are now returning from the southern area. Two enemy destroyers have been reported to be headed for Kiska.

October 19   The B-26's, etc., beat us to them. Both destroyers were sunk, one B-26 was shot down. The destroyers carried crated planes on their decks.

October 25   Arrived at Dutch Harbor on Unalaska. *Nashville* has left us. At 1300 we got underway. Sea so rough, our destroyer escort can't keep up with us. Headed for 'Frisco at 18 knots (no wonder). Record rolls of 35 degrees.

Chapter Nine

U SS St. Louis, now with the title "the U.S. Navy's most traveled ship," heads for home.

The Roosevelt Administration, up to this time, had given young men a choice of employment through either the C.C.C. (Civilian Conservation Corp), or the N.Y.A. (National Youth Administration), but now the draft had become a bit popular.

In the southwestern corner of Pennsylvania lies a small coal-mining town of Marianna. Towns like this, as well as small farming communities and others throughout the nation, which would be furnishing the young men to fight this ugly war.

From the newspaper accounts of the action in the Pacific, it sounded like it just couldn't last too much longer, but to a long tall lad by the name of Larry Fridley, the war was just beginning, as he found out later. He had finished a course in welding through the N.Y.A. and had a job offer with the Sun Shipbuilding Company, in Chester, PA.

Larry decided he would rather sail the ships than make them, so on September 5, 1942, he enlisted in the Navy at Morgantown, West Virginia.

Three days later, Larry left home for the Navy, was sworn in on the 9th of September, and arrived at Great Lakes Naval Training Station on the 10th.

Something amusing happened to Larry while changing from civilian clothes into the Navy wrap; while he was going through the issue line, they asked what size coat he would be wearing. At slightly over 6'4" tall, weighing about 155 pounds, Larry thought a size 36 peacoat would have more than ample room for his frame. They threw him a size 44, which almost knocked him over. Larry looked at the peacoat, and remarked that it was a size 44. They replied, "Keep moving sailor, you will grow into it." Larry simply looked at it and shook his head. It looked like an awful lot to grow into.

The food was quite different, but there was plenty of it as Company 996 started its boot camp training. First, you had to learn to jump in order to get from the truck that hauled the new recruits to the barracks. Of course, these were newly built barracks with narrow planks stretching from the road to the buildings. Jumping and balancing oneself on the planks was the first part of the training, whether they realized it or not.

Why they called it Green Bay was a mystery, as nothing even resembled the color green.

They must have needed bodies on the front lines, because Larry was headed home on a nine day leave just one month to the day that he arrived at boot camp. After returning from boot leave, Larry left O.G.U. (Out Going Unit) in Great Lakes for Treasure Island, California.

The post-boot camp training was the endurance ride cross-country on the train called The Challenger. It really was a challenge. Arriving at Treasure Island, California, on the 23rd of October, Larry was the farthest away from home he had ever been and living on an island already.

Then on the 5th of November, Larry and six other men from Company 996 were assigned to the light cruiser USS St. Louis, with the number 49 on her bow.

Larry's second time on the water was from Treasure Island up to Mare Island, where the drafts were split-up when each ship sent their transportation.

Here in the dry-dock was this big metal monster Larry had been assigned, and he was soon aboard. He hadn't known what being homesick really was until this day. The ship had just come back from Alaska, where she had been assigned to killing and chasing Japs, after being chased herself on December 7th from Pearl Harbor.

Chapter Nine

Everything on topside was a terrible mess, as it always was in port. Gear of all sorts lay scattered throughout the entire area of the deck. With bag and baggage, Larry muscled his way up the gangway, finding himself face to face with a keen-eyed, rough-and-tough boatswain mate. The boatswain was probably thinking to himself, "How bad can things get?" when he saw this draft.

The first order was to drop the baggage and fall in for another regulation muster. "Put out all those cigarettes! Square your hats! Keep it quiet during this muster!" The words were shouted out from between his upper and lower molars in an unwelcoming tone of voice. He resembled a dehydrated Swede and acted like a fullback with his own interference; he also figured each man came into the Navy to do his bit—the least bit possible. After a 4.0 muster, he then told them they were all in a division of their own, called X division.

A good chow was next on the list, which everyone figured he had earned, even though it had just been a day of waiting and mustering and carrying luggage. Before some were through eating, they began to realize that they must be in an important division to be called upon so much. It was, "Five men from the X-division report to the fantail for working party." "Seven men from X-division report to the foscle." "X-division draw your hammocks in compartment C-301-L." This was just breaking them in, as it went on for days.

Waiting in the mess hall later, Larry recognized the six original men from his own company at boot camp. A little, stocky, comical sailor with a guitar happened to be the center of attention. Charles (Happy) Dunham had been in Company 996 with Larry and hailed from a place called Chilicothe, Ohio. He specialized in songs such as "The Little Ball of Yarn," "I'm a Draftee," "I Had but Fifty Cents," and "Never Trust a Sailor." For that type of music, Dunham was without a doubt hard to beat. Anyone who heard those songs would have probably said to themselves, "Well life isn't so bad after all," and it really wasn't when Dunham picked these out on his juke box. He was the life of the party, and Larry was proud to learn that there was such talent in his rebel-like company.

Dunham's popularity surged when he changed his music to the lonely, hillbilly style. His performances would bring tears, and when it became too much for Larry he would leave and head topside to find a quiet place alone on the fantail looking across the bay to Vallejo. He would reminisce on his civilian days, wondering why he joined such an outfit, and why he left a good home. After taking it all in, Larry would sometimes decide, "Tomorrow I'll leave." Of course, "tomorrow" never did come.

Larry found it amazing that this ship, the one he was now standing on, was at Pearl Harbor on the day of the attack and had escaped unharmed, and then had gone on to Alaska to fight the rice-paddy boys and chased them to within 500 miles of their home. Larry overheard some old salts talking to some fresh boots regarding this. The boots all knew this would probably be their home for quite some time and were now interested in obtaining the data on the big monster.

Larry at the age of 18 was very proud of his new fifteen million dollar home. After chipping paint for a week in this X-division, Larry's draft was assembled on the fantail for classification. This was supposedly to direct them to the division aboard ship which they would be best suited.

These forms that were handed to them were to be filled out mostly pertaining to the occupation that they had in civilian life. Larry didn't know which job he would prefer aboard this beast of steel, but he did realize that chipping paint can get very monotonous. To eliminate this, Larry decided to put down his welding experience, not knowing where this would put him aboard ship. It didn't matter too much because Larry found himself in the Black Gang the next day.

The Black Gang is the navy engineer force—the men who work below deck in the machinery department of the ships. They have an uncanny knack for turning from white to black. Below deck, it's just a matter of minutes before faces become stained, and arms and torsos grimy. The members of the Black Gang never really feel at home unless they're covered with perspiration and deafened by noise. Ashore, the non-rated men of the Black Gang can be identified, not by the dirt and grime, but by the red stripe on the left shoulder seam of their jumper.

Dunham and Finnerin, two of Larry's buddies from boot camp, informed him that they were now in the B-division. Curious as to

Chapter Nine

what the B-division was, Larry looked around the deck for one of the plank owners (sailors who commissioned the ship). Easing back toward the number five gun turret, he said, "Hey Mack, what does B-division mean?" In a voice of close similarity to a boatswain mate, the gunner said, "Buddy, you're in a good division. 'B' means you'll be here when we leave and be here when we get back." That sounded good, but not authentic. Just about that time, Chief Watertender Sprinkle arrived on the scene and said, "Sailors, do you know where number two fireroom is located?" Three faces stared first at each other, then back at him, saying, "What did you say sir?"

It seemed that all chiefs hated to be called sir, but Chief Sprinkle hated it a little bit more than the ordinary chief. With a mean look and a few harsh words, he said, "I'll meet you sailors at the entrance of number two fireroom in about ten minutes." Dunham had already been ordered to report somewhere in ten minutes, so he took off, thinking to himself, "Well, that's all taken care of now." This left Larry and Finnerin alone, asking each other, "What did that Chief say?" Moving down across the second deck, hoping they would run into the chief at the right spot, they suddenly found a long line of sailors. "Maybe this is it?" said Finnerin. "No," Larry replied, "they're selling tomato juice here. Shall we get one?" Finnerin replied, "No, the line is too long." They were standing there, debating, when who should arrive but Chief Sprinkle himself. From the top of his lungs, he let out a yell, "I knew I would find you here! Why didn't you go where I told you?!" Larry and Finnerin had no time to answer before, "Well, wise guys, just come along with me and I'll see that you get where I want you."

At the center of the mess hall on the starboard side of the third deck, there was an entrance with a ladder that descended down two more decks. As Larry and Finnerin peered down the ladder, the chief's voice resounded, "Come on! Let's get moving, don't stand there and look at yourselves." The chief took the lead down the long ladder, opening a door which created a draft almost strong enough to lift them back up to the top. The draft wasn't as bad as the noise which the big blowers were making inside the door. Once inside, neither Finnerin nor Larry could hear a word the chief said. In the loudest tone he could muster, he told them to look the place over and get acquainted with the noise.

Larry had decided from the minute he stopped his foot in the operating space that he hated it, and would rather be up where he could see things and feel the effects of the fresh air. Everything seemed crowded to them, and with four big boilers—which put out over 500 pounds of steam—and about twelve pumps and the blowers, it couldn't help but be crowded. The space in the center from which the boilers were fired and controlled was called the operating space. This one, placed back in the after part of the ship, was identified as the number II boiler operating space (B.O.S.). In the forward portion of the ship, they had the same setup, and it was known as the number I boiler operating space (B.O.S.). Connecting these operating spaces on both sides were watertight doors, which lead to enclosed compartments which were very, very hot during times of operation—also known as firerooms.

On *St. Louis*, which was the sister ship to the USS Helena (CL-50), the order of engineering spaces started forward—forward diesel, number I B.O.S., forward engine room, after or number II B.O.S., after engine room (which was the control station), the after diesel, and ended with the shaft alleys.

These different stations made up the engineering or artificer branch of the ship. Also included with these stations are the electrical work shops, machine shops, tool issuing rooms and oil shacks.

While Finnerin and Larry were obtaining these instructions, Dunham showed up. After a little review, they made sure they knew where to return the following morning, and the water-tender in charge let them secure for the day. They could now go back to their lockers, which was usually a big sea-bag. Larry had rigged up a mattress cover with about five knots tied in it. This, of course, kept the thieves out, providing they didn't want to be too rough and cut holes through it.

Part of the draft had been assigned a regular compartment to keep their gear in, but Larry and Finnerin had just left theirs where they thought it would be most convenient to find. This was somewhere near the engineering living compartment. Larry chased back and forth throughout the ship, looking for his big, old mattress cover which had the necessary equipment for shaving, taking a shower, and changing

Chapter Nine

to a cleaner uniform. To make matters more complicated, very few had been issued bunks in which to sleep, so Larry and Finnerin were tricing theirs up in the mess hall. After a few nights of taking this and everything else into consideration, Larry was racking his brain trying to figure out some way to get out of such an outfit.

With slight pain in his kidneys as a result of the saggy hammock, Larry went to the sick bay hoping to get out of the Navy from kidney trouble. He told the doctor it bothered him so very much that the doctor had him urinate in a bottle. He was allowed to take it into the private head. He had the idea of adding water, but figured maybe he did have bad kidneys and it would show without the use of anything. They took the sample and told Larry they would call him if anything was wrong. Two days passed with no call, so Larry decided to try again—this time adding water. This time, he told the story to the pharmacist mate on duty, and another sample was taken, to which he added the water. Larry still didn't receive an answer for this, so he gave up, with the idea that he was now in the Navy for good.

The idea of liberty hadn't struck Larry's mind until now, when he was totally disgusted. He had heard some tall stories from the old salts down below which had gotten him even more excited for the reprieve, but Larry would need to retrieve his liberty card first. There were so many different faces aboard ship, Larry had a difficult time deciding just who should be called "sir." That evening, he went to the fireman on cold iron watch and said, "Sir, do you know who has my liberty card?" The poor guy stared back at him and said, "No sir, but you could try the log room."

When he got to the log room, they told him the liberty petty officer had them. "Now I wonder what his name could be, I'll just go back down to the compartment and see what the hell is wrong around here," Larry thought. Luckily enough, he arrived just in time to catch the petty officer who had the cards, and in a short while Larry was on his way.

He might have been on his way, but only to the quarterdeck, where he was checked by the officer of the deck (O.O.D.). The officer took one look at him and said, "Sailor, you better go back and shine those shoes." This made Larry very angry, now hating everything that resembled an officer. Down in the living compartment,

Larry broke into a sweat trying to get his oil-smeared shoes to shine. He used matches to burn off the oil, and shaving lotion to give them that "added something," but they still didn't have much of a shine. "Oh well, I'll try it again and if he says anything, I'll tell him I'm a fireman," Larry concluded. Wiping the sweat from his brow as he reached topside, he again approached the officer, who told him, "If you want to go ashore, you'll have to have on another neckerchief, sailor." Larry was now so mad that he couldn't even begin to put together the words he wanted to say. If he could have put his words together for the officer, he would have spent his first cruise in the brig. Larry now figured that there was only one solution—to borrow a neckerchief from someone. On his way back, Larry passed mount five, feeling very sure of himself—that is, until he hit a stanchion and almost knocked himself out. At this point, he almost felt like jumping over the side of the ship, but decided to give it one last try. The officer must have realized how optimistic this kid really was, because he granted permission this time. Larry could have broken the gangway, trying to get off before he changed his mind.

Larry, not knowing his way around, followed the crowd, which took him to the ferry landing. In just a few minutes, he was on Georgia Street in Vallejo, which was a prosperous little city at the time.

It felt natural for Larry to walk down skid row and see what was clicking in the line of good liberty. He had found out beforehand that skid row was a place to meet high heels, low heels, and just ordinary heels. This particular skid row, like any other, had its share of gin-joints which attracted the attention of Larry as well as the rest of the crowd. He made the tour a couple of times before acquiring the nerve to enter one, owing to the fact that he was only eighteen years of age. He was usually able to pass for twenty-one on his height. When he was once there, he hesitated to leave and try another because of his age, and he figured that the drinks weren't bad there, so why bother. His first liberty was just about like it would be for most any other boot arriving aboard their first ship. Although this wasn't the kind of liberty Larry had expected, he also wasn't exactly in any big hurry to return to the fifteen million dollar home of his over in the shipyard. This could have been the mistake that would make him a restricted man or even a P.A.L.

Chapter Nine

Larry didn't know that there was a liberty card box on the quarterdeck for deposit of his card upon returning aboard ship. It was about 0300 that morning when, with a lot of luck, Larry found his sack and was sleeping within minutes like a sailor just getting off the 12-4 watch. When he awakened, it was too late for chow and even late for mustering on station, but he managed to get the card in by the skin of his teeth.

The old routine below decks was now becoming a process of cleaning up and getting ready for the yard test of machinery. Larry and the gang would gather behind the boilers and start their bull sessions. Sometimes it would even be so interesting that the petty officer himself would join in on the conversations.

These conversations were supposed to have been the true tales from the night before or that morning. Larry was starting to pick up on this. When they asked him what he did on his first liberty, he said, "Fellows, part of my money went for liquor, part for women, and the rest I just spent foolishly." It wasn't many liberties though until he could also shoot the breezes about this new era in his life. Back aboard *St. Louis*, it was time for a change of skippers.

Captain Rood had just given his farewell speech and proceeded to the gangway. It appeared he had tears in his eyes; he wasn't the only one. Most everyone, including the newcomers, were affected.

The question now was whether the ship could get another skipper equal to the one who had just departed. This was something that each man would determine for himself. Only time would tell, but he would turn out to be a gentleman, thoroughly familiar with the many sides of his profession, who enjoyed the confidence and admiration of the men whom he commanded.

Captain Colin Campbell entered the Naval Academy from Kansas, where his father practiced law. In Europe during the '14 midshipman cruise, he felt the rumbling of the World War that was to see his class graduated prematurely in 1917. While on the North Dakota, he was promoted to a junior grade lieutenant eleven months after midshipmen.

When the first World War ended, he went to Asiatic station on the shakedown cruise of the destroyer USS Chandler (DD206) and stayed to command USS Avoset (AM19). Then a lieutenant, he served as executive officer of the destroyer USS Southard (DD207), before going to the old Bureau of Engineering for his first tour of shore duty.

For his three years as executive officer of USS Sharkey (DD281), he served on European station that included duty in the Baltic and at Gravesend. Upon conclusion of this tour of sea duty, Captain Campbell was selected to study law at George Washington University where he received his ILB degree in 1931.

As Admiral Leahy's flag secretary, he oversaw the operations of destroyers from USS Raleigh (CL7), and continued on that post when Leahy was relieved by Admiral Watson.

In 1934, his legal training saw practical use as an aide to the Judge Advocate General. Said the captain of his tenure, "I was the man at the front desk."

1937 found Captain Campbell navigating USS New Mexico (BB40), until his appointment as commanding officer of the USS Hannibal (AG1). Ashore on his next tour of duty, he acted as personnel and legal officer of the Twelfth Naval District in San Francisco.

After serving as the executive officer of the USS Tennessee (BB43), Captain Campbell was chosen to command the USS Whitney (AD4), which he left in November 1942 to become the skipper of *St. Louis*.

Captain Colin Campbell

Chapter Nine

Captain Colin Campbell

Christmas was now only a few weeks off and the ship was being finished at the yard. Larry had been making his routine liberties in Vallejo. He had talked many times of going to Frisco and Oakland, but could never seem to leave Vallejo. He was being taken for his money, and enjoying every moment of it, like so many other thousands which made the city so prosperous.

The ship was awaiting orders which were due any day. When they finally arrived, *St. Louis* was now to sail on December 3rd for the South Pacific.

Liberty was granted on the 2nd and Larry made full use of it. He went ashore very sad, and the little city had now put up their Christmas trimmings. The Christmas songs were being played on the jukeboxes. This was the first time Larry had heard the song "White Christmas," and it would make an impression on his mind which he would never forget. He stayed in the little town until 0500 when all hands were called back to the ship due to a strange ship off the coast.

The Saga of the Lucky Lou

"I Had but Fifty Cents"
I took my girl to a fancy ball.
It was an associable hop.
We danced until the folks went home.
And the music had to stop.

Then to a restaurant we went,
The best one on the street.
She said she wasn't hungry, boys,
But this is what she'd eat:
A dozen of raw, a plate of slaw, a chicken and a roast.
Some asparagus, and applesauce, and soft-shelled crab and toast.
Irish stew, and crackers too, her appetite was immense.
When she called for a pie, I thought I'd die,
because I had but fifty cents.

Now she said she wasn't thirsty boys,
She didn't care to drink.
But you can bet your only pair of pants,
That she cannot be beat.
A glass of ale, a gin cocktail, she made me shake with fear.
A ginger pop with rum on top, and then a glass of beer.
When she asked for more, I fell to the floor
because I had but fifty cents.

Today I'm a tired, wearied fireman.
Been down in the fireroom all day.
Cleaning firesides and bilges.
Preparing to get underway.

Now the hand-holes and manholes are fitted tightly,
Fitted tightly with gaskets, you see.
Just getting everything ready
To take a trip out to sea.

Chapter Nine

> Now the machinery is neatly polished,
> The shit-can is empty you see.
> And the words of Gallagan,
> Were meant for the fireman,
> To take it with ease.
>
> We're getting underway Tuesday,
> Underway for Frisco, you see.
> And we all hope the girls there are waiting,
> To go on the first liberty.
> Composed by Dunham and Larry.

Under ordinary conditions at sea:

0345	Relieve the watch.
0500	Reveille. Call all hands. Light the smoking lamp.
0520	Pipe sweepers.
0530	Turn to. Smoking lamp out. Execute morning orders.
0715	Trice up all hammocks. Light smoking lamp.
0730	Breakfast.
0745	Relieve the watch.
0800	Turn to. Smoking lamp out.
0830	Sick call.
0910	Officer's call. Divisions fall in for quarters.
0915	Quarters for muster and inspection.
1130	Early chow for oncoming watch.
1145	Relieve the watch.
1200	Dinner.
1300	Turn to. Pipe sweepers. Smoking lamp out.
1545	Relieve the watch.
1630	Sweep down. Knock off ships work. Light smoking lamp.
1700	Clear up decks.
1715	Mess gear.
1730	Supper- relieve the watch for chow.
1830	Clean sweep down fore and aft.
1900	Movies (conditions prevailing).

1930	Hammocks (no smoking below decks).
1945	Relieve the watch.
2100	Smoking lamp out. Turn out lights. Taps.
2330	Call the mid-watch.
2345	Relieve the watch.

Chapter Ten

December 3rd found the ships crew on all their stations early, prepared to get underway, this time for a number of months. On topside it was busy, and down below it was a madhouse, but this was natural. It was hot; the noise of the blowers and pumps was terrific. The hatches were now being dogged. Like a baby's bladder, it was water-tight integrity.

Now under pressure in the operating spaces, Larry has on the J.V. phones. He didn't have time to think about what might be going on topside.

Larry, already on his first ship, was on his first cruise and with a new skipper. When he got off watch, the first place he headed was to grab a bite at chow before heading topside. Air is what he wanted, good fresh air, not the artificial quality of air he had been breathing for four hours. When he finally reached the main deck, it seemed as if the ship might be rolling a bit. Like many of the others, he was beginning to get dizzy. Some were worse off, and for a moment it seemed that Larry might follow in their footsteps, but he kept moving around and by some strange luck managed to escape seasickness.

Between the watches, sailors were usually drawing something or handing something in. The old saying was "all men having none, draw one, and all men having two, turn one in."

The watches in the boiler operating spaces usually consisted of ten men and a chief. One fireman for each of the four boilers, one on the J.V. phones, a messenger, and two water-tenders on the checks which control the water fed to the boilers. There were two water-tenders on the throttles for controlling the air pressure, and last, but not least, there was the chief water-tender who was in charge of the watch.

The fireman who are assigned to the boilers are responsible for cleaning each of the nine burners in each boiler upon relieving the watch. After this operation, the fireman then wiped up all the oil around the outside of the boiler to prevent fire hazard. The boilers were controlled by two systems, the split system and the open system.

The split system was the one in which the forward boilers were separated from the after boilers, and one fireman would be assigned to the control boiler for forward, while another was assigned to the control boiler aft. These firemen tell their partners on the corresponding boilers how many burners they should have lit, and just what oil pressure they need to keep the steam at the designated pressure—which was 565 pounds, being of superheated steam.

One hour before sunrise every morning, the boiler tubes had to be blown and the same thing had to be done every night one hour after sunset. The soot from this operation discouraged the deck force very much, many times ruining some poor old boatswain mates paint job.

This operation didn't only mean dirt on topside, but it meant work for the men below, as all hands cooperated except the phone talker; his sole aim was to get the correct orders, and to report the correct answers to the man on the control board in the after engine room.

The evaporators were now short of personnel and that meant a selection among the new firemen. When the chiefs reached a decision, it was Larry who had been chosen for the job. The first thing to discourage him was the temperatures under which he had to work; it was many, many times worse than the operating space.

The first class petty officer gave him all the dope on how to stand an evaporator watch, in only one easy lesson. That was what the petty officer figured, but Larry didn't catch on that easy, in fact, he didn't even catch on. This gentleman, with over thirteen years experience, knew his job and he knew it well. He went on to tell Larry

Chapter Ten

the names of all the pumps, explaining every motion it made and what it did. He told him to watch the water level at the side of the evaporators in the meantime, to be sure and switch the 150 gallon tanks when they got full, and to take the readings every hour on the hour. By this time, Larry was wet with perspiration, and when his boss asked if he thought he could handle it, he said, "Yes!" in a hurry so as to get rid of him.

As soon as he left, Larry immediately took off his shirt, then he looked around and heard water flowing into the bilges. This frightened him and he started to leave, before miraculously recalling that the tank was to be switched over when it filled up. Larry had gotten his first task correct. "Oh my, still no cooler and I've got my shirt off and am standing under a blower," Larry thought. The water was now unequal in the evaporators, so he got to work turning the valves, "turn one left, turn one right," the motto he muttered as he worked. Looking at his timepiece, Larry saw that it was already ten minutes past the hour. "Oh no, shall I take the readings now, or wait 'till the next reading comes up?! Oh, I had better take them now." He tried to do it hurriedly under the blower, but the blower kept blowing away the paper on which he was trying to write. Even though Larry was a pretty good writer, the log looked like a Chinese checkerboard. When he got through with the log, he glanced down to see where the water level was in the sightglass, but couldn't see it. "Now, where in the hell could it be? At the top or at the bottom?" Larry thought. "If I remember right, it was low the last time I saw it, so it's probably at the bottom. Oh well, I'll open the valve a little more and see what happens." He gave the valve a couple more turns, and with good guessing and a little bit of luck he got the water up to where he could see it.

"Let's see know, what did he say about that damn steam valve over there? I forgot. It isn't making any noise, so I guess it's all right. Just who in the hell does he think I am anyway? At this rate, I should be the chief engineer by the time we reach our first port. Man, it's so ugly hot, I think I'll take off my pants; they're all soaked and wet anyways. I'll just hang them up to dry for a while." Larry took off his dungarees and hung them up to dry while he started to take the hourly readings again. It was too much to bother with the blower again, so he sat down on the sand box and started to radio the log. Finally contented, the steam trap lifted suddenly and violently on one of the valve lines. Larry jumped two feet in the air and immediately started for the hatch. As he started to pass through the entrance, he bumped square into Hebert, his boss, and was so shaken that he couldn't even explain why he was leaving. Hebert turned him around, steered him back towards the boilers, and made him fight his way through the steam back to the valve, which he soon had fixed. Now he was to catch hell. "I thought I told you to watch that valve! Just take a look at that water level! Where is it?!" Hebert demanded. "I don't know," Larry mumbled in a shaky voice. "Why don't you know? Where in the hell do you think you are, back in school?" Hebert responded. He hung around with him for the rest of the watch and raised all hell the entire time. Before Larry was relieved of the watch, it was also his job to empty the trash cans. With a can in one hand and a sack in the other, he maneuvered topside, just missing the officers mess room since the evaporators were forward of officers quarters.

Reaching topside just forward of mount four, Larry found it as black as raven feathers and very rough and windy. He paused a few minutes before feeling his way aft to the fantail. The wind was blowing fiercely, the waves large and furious. He tripped twice, and felt like throwing the garbage over the side, but continued to press his way through to the fantail. As he dumped the trash, he looked at the long, wide wake the old cruiser screws were leaving behind them. The first of the raindrops began pelting, and then the downpour began. Not a person could be seen, except those rigging up shelter as they were standing watch on the guns. Larry was again thinking that he would rather be in the deck force than where he was with that soup-head boss of his, but he felt sorry for the guys who were on the guns in these rough conditions while he was below deck and warm—albeit very, very warm. Larry headed towards the sleeping quarters where his hammock was strung, removed his wet clothing, and climbed in the sack. "What a helluva thing the Navy thought of to sleep in," he thought as he climbed in. Despite this, it still felt good after standing one of those damned evaporator watches.

The next day, Larry reported to his station on watch, totally

Chapter Ten

disgusted and not giving a damn if he ever made any more water. Again, Hebert started raising hell, and it started to arouse Larry's temper. At this, Hebert took the listening end as Larry told him just what he really thought of him and the evaporators.

Hebert told him he would be transferred to the deck force in just a few days, to which Larry replied that he would much rather be up there than where he was. The following day during general quarters, the chief in charge of the evaporators questioned Larry, and he received the same response. After these exchanges were relayed to the chief in the operating space, Larry was given his old job back. This was the turning point in Larry's life as a sailor; from then on, he was a hard worker, and very eager to learn the trade.

Gambling was now becoming ordinary entertainment. Larry had been pretty good at handling the cards during black jack while on the outside, and now he could hardly wait till payday. When payday did arrive, he quickly wished it hadn't. With a crowd of about seven squatting partners, Larry laid his greenback on the deck. He received his two cards. He decided to sleep on the dealer, thinking "why not?" since he only had a tray showing and Larry had nothing more than a measly fifteen. Yes, Larry had it figured out all right, because the dealer did have a hard-hitting thirteen, but he took the next card which gave him a total of twenty. The other boys just laughed this off, but then came the second hand, and Larry got beat again. "Just what the hell comes off here anyway? I had better start playing black jack instead of sleeping here on my sweet sixteens." Larry thought. The third hand was dealt, and again he decided to squeeze this one, hoping for a twenty at least. "What do you know! Two big queens right together! What did I hear, someone say black jack?! No, it's just the dealer getting the jack of diamonds and the ace of spades." This was three straight losses, and it made him look like a boot at the profession. He was now cursing with every word in the foul language dictionary. Larry changed positions, hoping this would change his luck, only to have another loss.

At this point, he decided to take one more crack at it, and if he lost, he would never again gamble aboard the ship. That's just what happened. Five losses in a row, and Larry swore off gambling right then and there. Never again did it bother him to watch others transfer those cabbage leaves back and forth. He realized that it was against the rules anyway, and could be hard on him if he ever got caught. This was a lesson one couldn't learn in school.

The "hammocks"—basically glorified canvas sacks—were still giving the newcomers problems. Finnerin and Larry always slept side by side, but tonight Finnerin wasn't holding his balance very well and swung over against him. Larry saw Finnerin almost hit the deck, and hoped he wouldn't have to abandon his own hammock. Finnerin tried to correct but wasn't on an even keel, and hit the deck with a terrific noise which sounded like Joe Louis dropping one of his heaviest opponents. Larry was now laughing strenuously, but then realized that Finnerin might have hurt himself, which he had. Finnerin's back was now hurting very much, so they decided to sleep this one out on the deck. The vibrations of the ship made this a very nauseating prospect, but this was the way they slept until assigned their bunks in the engineering department some weeks later.

Day by day, the ship was approaching "the line." "Crossing the Line" is the term used by the Navy for a ship crossing the Equator, and all of the ceremonies that come with it. It was December 11th, and *St. Louis* was now crossing the Equator. At that time, all hands that hadn't previously made the crossing were initiated into the "Ancient Order of the Deep." These characters were called "pollywogs" until they were initiated, at which time they became "shellbacks."

The ceremony is an ancient ritual of all mariners, dating back to the Middle Ages. In those days, however, it was not performed upon crossing the Equator, but upon reaching tropical waters and crossing the Arctic Circle. The initiation at that time consisted of throwing the pollywog into the sea from the yardarm, unless he gave money to the older sailors. The present-day ritual is a direct descendent of this ancient custom.

True to tradition, as *St. Louis* neared the Equator, preparations were begun to receive King Neptune and his royal court.

The day before the crossing, all pollywogs were called to the quarterdeck to receive their subpoenas from "Davy Jones," who would relay that he had come aboard some time during the night. Davy was a piratical-looking figure with boots, ragged trousers, a black patch over one eye, and long flowing hair and beard. Upon

Chapter Ten

receiving their subpoena from Davy Jones, each pollywog learned that he was ordered to appear the next day before his Imperial Highness, Neptunus Rex, Ruler of the Raging Main, to answer a specific charge.

King Neptune

The following morning, after an uneasy chow, the pollywogs were called topside where they caught their first glimpse of His Royal Highness, the Queen, and the court. With a fanfare provided by the royal trumpeter, the court would inspect the ship, and then move to the fantail where the "courtroom" had been set up. The trials then commenced.

Before appearing before the court, the pollywog was "prepared" by being forced to crawl through a low, canvas tunnel, the bottom consisting of loose potatoes. The men were helped through by a heavy stream of salt water from a fire hose held by a man at the entrance, and greeted by another hose at the exit of the tunnel. He was made to keep his head down by the continuous use of paddles wielded over the top of the tunnel by over-enthusiastic paddlers.

After completing this hazardous journey through the tunnel, the victim emerged only to be met by a handful of flour thrown in his face. He was then taken in hand by the royal chief of police and

The Saga of the Lucky Lou

guided to the royal scribe who read the charges against him. Upon hearing the charges, the pollywog was asked to enter the usual plea of guilty or not guilty. If he pleaded guilty, he was given the routine initiation. However, if he was foolhardy enough to answer not guilty, he was given special consideration.

After making his plea, the pollywog was led to the royal barber, who shaved the traditional Southern Cross in his hair. If he pleaded not guilty, the victim usually lost all of his hair.

Upon receiving the tonsorial treatment, the pollywog met the devil, who proved a very shocking spectacle with the help of his special, electrical pitchfork.

The hapless man was now rescued from the devil by Davy Jones who, with a few derogatory remarks, presented him to King Neptune. "His Salty Majesty" was a leathery, old gentleman with a golden crown, long white hair, a mustache, and a beard. As he approached the throne, the defendant was forced to pay homage to the king by bowing before him, whereupon the devil enlivened the scene with frequent jabs from his much-respected pitchfork.

The King would then ask the man the usual questions concerning his charges, hear his plea, and sentence him to entertain the court with a song and a dance. This dance was performed with the assistance of the devil and the royal jester.

Upon completing his sentence, he was then presented to the Queen, the royal princess, who was slightly more amorous, and was asked to hold the "royal baby." The "baby" would behave itself exactly as all babies do when being held by strangers.

The somewhat chagrined pollywog was then led before the royal chaplain, who listened to his tales of woe and blessed him by painting a large cross on his chest with blue paint, and putting a small cross of grease on his forehead.

After such strenuous activity, the man was taken to the royal doctor to be repaired. While lying on the operating table, the patient was suddenly aware of the fact that it was not at all comfortable due to the fact that it was also electrified. After telling the doctor about his aches and pains, the pollywog was liberally covered with mercurochrome and lubricating grease, and then sent on to the royal navigator.

Chapter Ten

The navigator, standing by a large reservoir of water on the quarterdeck, placed the pollywog in front of him with his back to the pool. After explaining the mysteries of ancient celestial navigation and kindred matters for a few minutes, the navigator would suddenly thrust a brush full of paint into the man's face. Involuntarily, the man would lean back to escape the paint and in so doing, find himself being thoroughly dunked by the bears standing in the tub. After being held under water until two-thirds drowned, he would then be brought back up and declared a shellback from that moment on. He could then remove the grease and watch the remainder of the initiation—if able.

What a day this was, and Larry declared that he would get even by participating in a line-crossing ceremony in the future to take revenge on future unfortunate pollywogs. Larry thought he had taken a beating in boot camp, and had lost a nice head of hair, but he had now lost all of his hair which just finished growing in nice and wavy. It was quite difficult to recognize some of the previous pollywogs now, with the Southern Cross cut through their hair, but the majority of these had gotten theirs cut and shaved as smooth as a baby's buttocks.

The big gripe aboard ship now was about the hot, tropical heat which was prevailing, torturing some worse than others, with heat rash breaking out all over the person's body. The ship's stores were kept busy trying to keep enough Mennen powder on hand, as this was most commonly used. Sailors were now sleeping topside at night, wearing only shorts and without a single blanket. This was rather a pleasant sleep at times, providing that it didn't rain, and Larry had begun to make it a habit. He had also begun to acquire quite a bronze look by now, which he joked could have been blamed on the heat radiating from the boilers, except that it was hotter topside in the sun than it was below.

Larry had read books and seen movies back home about the beautiful South Sea Island paradises, and their mild and adaptable climate, as well as the beautiful grass-skirted senoritas.

The ship was now heading for operation in this area, and with overwhelming anticipation the days were being accurately counted, considering the change in time which was set forth in crossing the

International Date Line on December 17, 1942.

Almost three weeks of direct sailing southward had slipped by, and the ship was now entering its first port, Noumea, New Caledonia (called White Lily). On the morning of the 18th day at sea, the ship was approaching the little atoll just before the island, visible in the background. With a clear blue sky and water to match, the sailors, who were getting their first glimpse of the green-palmed island, began to think that they were truly about to take their liberty in Paradise.

As the ship moved closer, things began to look bare and the hills were becoming numerous. When they finally rounded the point, the little town of Noumea came into view. To its left appeared another little village, which turned out to be the leper colony. The ship had now come to a rest in the water, and sailors strolled the deck trying to get their viewpoint on the liberty: "Oh boy, this really looks nice and green and fresh, and the women are probably the same!"

Everyone was now waiting for liberty call to be announced, but this was a great surprise. There weren't many ships in the harbor as yet, but they had strict orders on the liberty, as it was not the place it appeared to be from out in the bay.

Instead, preparations were now being made to clean up the ship, since Christmas was only four days off. The crew had gone all-out to prepare for a fine, well-cleaned ship for their captain on Christmas Day. After these four days of hard work and preparations for the holiday entertainment which was to be held aboard ship, part of the crew was now to be granted liberty. The liberty party consisted of only a few petty officers from each division, so this eliminated Larry, but he didn't mind after hearing what the liberty was like and what prevailed on the small island.

Liberty was now granted on Christmas Day, and the happy hour took place in the afternoon with all hands shifting into the uniform of the day, which was whites. They weren't exactly free of wrinkles, but they were clean.

The liberty party made the liberty landing at Noumea and hit the town, of course, looking for some evil spirits and perhaps a Hedy Lamour or Gene Tierney—a fair young damsel to sweep them off their feet. Like any place on earth where there are inhabitants,

Chapter Ten

there is some sort of liquid spirits available, but the latter issue was more complicated, as the French inhabitants knew of their expected arrival and had hidden the fairer sex up in the hills.

The leper colony was also now clearly visible, and it was a spooky-looking place with its houses, gardens, and little tiny chapel. The brightly-colored flowers and tropical plants gave the colony its life and noticeable attention. A few cattle roamed the side of the hills surrounding the colony.

On the street corners were the dark-skinned, red-headed natives, with their souvenirs, repeating the words, "one dolla!" or, "one dolla-half!" After a purchase of souvenirs and a chat with these brown creatures, who "no-speak-a-the-English" but were trained students of hand signals, they then wandered over to the amusement center—a couple of overcrowded theaters.

The most interesting spot was the Army PX, where the sailors could obtain their gedunks (ice cream) and soft drinks. Of course, there were those who ventured out-of-bounds and would secure a bottle by paying three or four times its original price. Money never means anything to a sailor while overseas, and the petty-officers had it to spare on this occasion. Examples were to be made by the top-ranking petty officers, and they were—examples of wrongdoing. The happy hour had to be interrupted to make room for the aviation crane to hoist up one stiff who was under the influence so bad that he couldn't climb the aviation ladder. Others struggled and made it, but this character, a first class petty officer, couldn't move a muscle.

The performance aboard ship on this Christmas Day were extraordinary, and after watching a few acts, the sailors would have advised the Mills Brothers that these vocals would make them look sick. The ad-libbing would send Abbott and Costello into the unknown. As for music, well Glenn Miller and Stan Kenton would no longer be favorites after seeing this orchestra in action. Many outside spectators were present, as the harbor had received a number of ships for a rest on this Christmas Day. The audience, aroused by the great performances, was almost hysterical now, when the show was interrupted momentarily to hoist this stiff aboard in a net. The sailor, being a typical sea-going rascal with every bit of the roughness and weight to make a nice sag in the net, was not officially logged on board. From the net, he was carried off in a stretcher to his bunk, and on went the shows.

Christmas Day aboard had started out with a clean, regulation ship, to be followed shortly with devotional services and a very delicious, appetizing dinner, as their slogan now was: "Eat hardy lads, and give the ship a good name." After dinner, liberty was granted to the fortunate ones, and last but not least came the great performances which went to make as nice a Christmas as one could expect overseas.

The morning of the 27th saw the ship getting up steam and weighing anchor early. The ship was now moving very slowly, making preparations to turn around in the bay. This procedure was a slow one, and the crew had now begun to criticize the skipper, wondering if he was just holding a drill or really meant to get underway. This being Captain Campbell's first cruiser experience may have had something to do with it. They began to get the impression that he wouldn't be able to maneuver his way out of trouble so well.

Larry was optimistic in this manner toward his captain and he believed he would take care of things as they arrived. The ship, now turned and facing the wide-open Pacific, was heading for another step-up the ladder in the line of action.

It was just a matter of three days sailing until they reached their next port, from which the Fleet would now operate. The turning point of the war in the Pacific had just taken place a couple of months beforehand. Guadalcanal was part of the fork-in-the-road which lead to victory, but it still wasn't officially declared ours until February 8, 1943.

Espirito was the port now where the ships were planning on operating from. The entrance to the bay was narrow, but kept stretching outward as the ships penetrated into it, and flanked on one side by Aore Island, the Navy base, and on the other side by the Army base, along with a few French inhabitants strung along the shore in small huts. The island was covered thickly with palm trees, very green in color.

Our troops had utilized their native trails, turning them into dirt roads which put up a dust thick enough to almost blind a sailor sitting on the fantail of his ship anchored halfway out into the bay.

Chapter Ten

On the opposite side, there was thickly covered jungle. This meant a battle for the whole fleet, as the ships would be stationed here and would need some sort of liberty or entertainment. This wasn't a battle where they used guns, but it was a battle in which manpower and machinery or tools was needed.

St. Louis was one of the first ships to send working parties to the beach, and Larry was among the group sent over the first day. As the small boat approached the shore, it reminded him of how he had read about the Marines landing in such places. The term "working party" fit this group very well, because it was all muscle work. Either you had them when you started or you would have them when you finished. Larry remembered how the gang back home used to scrape up enough money to buy coconuts for the shacks they would build; by now he had picked up so many that he wished they were still back there scraping up money for them.

This was also the kind of job that built up an appetite sufficient enough to cover two deluxe dinners anywhere; the boys went through a box of sandwiches like a litter of hungry mice. After the first day's work, there still didn't seem to be much progress; it felt to the sailors like a captain's inspection which one prepares for all week, after which he announces that the ship still looks terrible. The next day, another group would be sent over to battle the conglomeration of wildlife in the Pacific.

Only two of these parties had been sent over, and then on January 2nd, *St. Louis*, *Helena*, and *Nashville*, along with the destroyers USS Fletcher (DD445) and USS O'Bannon (DD450) under the command of Rear Admiral Walden L. Ainsworth, inaugurated the first series of bombardments by surface vessels.

The Saga of the Lucky Lou

Walden L. Ainsworth

0032 *Grayback* challenges *Nashville* (4000 yards ahead). Affirm received.
0035 *St. Louis* decreases speed to 13 knots.
0038 *Grayback* reported at 50 degrees, range 3500 yards.
0044 *Grayback* at 60 degrees relative, range 1000 yards.
0045 Coming on range for bombardment of the airfield.
0100 *Nashville* opens fire.
0111 *Nashville* ceased fire.

Chapter Eleven

Ainsworth had directed his vessels around the north end of Rendova Island where the submarine USS Grayback (SS208) had been waiting to act in the unaccustomed role of a sea buoy in those treacherous waters that black night of January 4, 1943. She had celebrated Christmas by adding four more enemy landing barges to her credit, which took place off the southern tip of New Georgia, but she was now to sail to Rendova and rescue a six-man crew of a B-26 which had crashed on the island.

The general quarters alarm was sounded at 2300. At 2315, there was radar contact eighteen miles south of the unit. At 2345, land was reported on starboard bow; *St. Louis'* speed was 26 knots. As the new day began on January 5, 1943, at 0015, "blackcats," or flares, were dropped on the target.

The time for attack was now growing nearer and nearer, and the ships in formation were about to let loose on Munda, which was covered with Japs. This was the first brush with action for Larry and many of the others, and the curiosity began to build their minds with each turn of the propeller's blade. Larry had his battle station in the Post Office compartment just slightly aft of the number two stack on the second deck. Classified as a boiler relief, he was a standby during action until relief was needed on one of the boilers down below.

This was a very important night, and even though it was past midnight, and his body was growing weaker from lack of sleep, he refused to let himself wander off into slumberland. Word had now been received by the phone talker that we were approaching the target at 24 knots, with land close on both sides, and *St. Louis* would be going in very close to the shore.

Larry was very anxious—more like scared stiff—and wondering just what was going to happen next.

Finally the moment had come, and at 0114, the big 5-inch guns let loose with a roar, and Larry would have sworn they were hit because of the vibrations and noises. Their speed was now 18 knots. Screws fell from the bulkheads, and pieces of light metal flew throughout the compartment. He, like the others, was crouched in the corner, holding his head and trying to protect himself.

After the first fire of the 5-inch, there was a slight pause which puzzled Larry very much. He figured once they let loose, it would be continuous firing from then on. Then the second 5-inch went off with a bang and there was another pause. After about three turns like this, Larry began to get mad and started asking some of the old salts, "Why the hell don't we go in there and slug it out with those sons-of-bitches?"

After having the situation explained to him, he still couldn't see why they were giving them time in between each firing. The idea was to fire and wait momentarily for a return, therefore assuring the ship that they had a good target. If there happens to be a return fire, then the challenge would be answered depending on the opposition.

It was the first engagement, and the first time Larry had heard the guns fired at the enemy. For Larry, though, it wasn't any fun because he couldn't see anything. He sat there listening, and shaking, and hoping that a shell or torpedo didn't penetrate that pig-iron thing.

After several rounds of 5 and 6-inch firing, it became monotonous crouching in one position the whole time. Larry moved over to an empty bunk and dropped into it. Adjusting himself, halfway between being asleep and being awake, he reminisced on his civilian days. At times, he would notice that there was no delay in firing and they were following one right after another. To this, Larry would smile from ear to ear, knowing that he was on one hell of a fighting ship. At 0124, *St. Louis* ceased fire.

Chapter Eleven

0125 *Helena* opens fire.
0135 *Helena* ceases fire.
0135 Our destroyers open fire. We expend 930 6-inch rounds.

Many Japs were killed, but this was only a warning, to let them know American ships were at hand, and not just for a visit. Larry said, "I can just see those rice-paddy boys on the waterfront, packing their bags and tents, heading for the hills or the jungle." He doubted that it would help them any, since these visits were going to become routine. From then on, they were going to be blown even from their hiding places.

0150 Destroyers cease fire.
0200 Flagship *Nashville* signaled, "Well done."
0215 Waiting on destroyers to catch up.
0245 Increased speed to 29 knots.
0930 Met other units. This was the cover-up force consisting of the cruisers *Honolulu, Achilles, Columbia, Louisville,* and four other destroyers.

Australian Cruiser - Achilles

The Saga of the Lucky Lou

Photographs taken of Munda on the morning of the 5th showed that the area had indeed been "thoroughly worked over." It had been the most destructible and efficient bombardment thrown at Jap installations up to that time.

The runways were a mess, a succession of overlapping shellholes from one end to the other. The enemy had lost a lot of stores and supplies, but the Americans were unsuccessful as far as putting the field out of operation. Twelve hours later, zeroes were taking off from Munda and looking for Admiral Ainsworth's ships.

1030   Ainsworth's ships, with the addition of the British cruiser Achilles, were steaming past Guadalcanal when attacked by six Jap dive-bombers. *St. Louis* was credited with shooting down three planes and *Helena* with one. *Honolulu* received two near misses. *Achilles* received one 100-pound bomb on top of her number three turret. It blew the top and portside off, killed nine men, injured eleven, and two were missing. *St. Louis* lost one scout plane while passing through Coral Sea; survivors were picked up by destroyers.

1830   *O'Bannon* attempted to pick up two Jap flyers. The pilot fired upon the rescuers so he was shot. The gunner was rescued, but died of wounds later.

1900   Units separated again to cover landing operations on Guadalcanal.

January 6   Steaming for Espirito. *Achilles* buried her dead.
January 7   Arrived at Espirito.
January 8   *St. Louis* is back at its base in Espirito.

This is the beginning of a long stretch of captain inspections. Even years later, Larry would never forget the first time he saw the captain. It was a Saturday inspection, he came to a halt and stared a hole clean through to the nape of his neck. "Square your hat," he said, eyes blazing with an incendiary fire and with a voice—though soft and quiet—strong enough to shake the keel of a battlewagon. Larry was scared, clean down to the bunion on his big toe. This was

Chapter Eleven

the first time he had heard him speak, and wanted it to be the last at such an occasion as this. Yes, Larry knew to have his hat squared at inspection, but he had been caught by surprise.

All hands went to quarters just before the time of inspection, and the captain would start forward and then work his way aft while inspecting the crew, but the divisions were usually at parade rest until he approached the vicinity. Larry got so excited when he heard the bugle sound for attention, he had forgotten the little white hat at the top of his head. Larry, being a little over 6'4", was the tallest in his division, and the divisions always lined up according to height, putting the tall fellow forward. This, of course, put him at the front of the first line so that he was always the first man to be inspected by the captain.

After he went down each aisle and inspected from a front view for haircuts, clean jumpers and trousers, skivvy shirts, shined shoes, and dog tags, he then got a view from the rear when the division officer gave the about turn.

After the week-end inspection, it was always out to sea again. On the night of January 24th, a similar and daring attack had been made on the field at Vila-Stanmore, on Kolombangara Island.

Admiral Ainsworth again took the cruisers *Nashville* and *Helena*, along with the destroyers *Nicholas, DeHaven, Radford,* and *O'Bannon*, in order to cause greater damage to the Japs than they suffered at Munda; nonetheless, they did not knock out the field. *St. Louis* was acting as a standby for the task group on this bombardment.

The rice-paddy boys were soon out with their shovels, road-scrapers, and everything else they had to patch the pitted fields back up. By nightfall, they were whole again.

This was discouraging, but Admiral Ainsworth had just begun what he intended on doing to the place. In spite of the constant bombing by American aircraft and bombardments by surface vessels, the Japs had gone right ahead and built two airfields.

Admiral Ainsworth knew he might destroy large quantities of gasoline and stores, as well as render the fields unusable during a critical time, but the only thing to do was to take the fields away from them completely, and Admiral Halsey had proposed to do just that.

Fleet Admiral William F. Halsey

St. Louis came back to Espirito, and again working parties were sent over to the beach to clear the thicket for future recreation. By this time, the other ships were of help in the task.

It was obvious now that their progress on the beach was picking up, and the natives began to gather around and help do the job—for a few shillings of course. They would bring their bags full of bananas, limes, and other tropical fruit down to the landing, but would hide their bag and just bring out a few things at a time to trade with the sailors. The sailors could have picked their own, but the natives had already taken care of it and were collecting quite the profit—a skivvy shirt or wrap of any kind felt good to them, as did the sugar, salt, and pepper which they were now using on their meals. No one ever actually saw them eating, but from the looks of some of them they did a lot of it. Aside from these trades with the sailors, the natives stayed scarce, moving their shacks deeper into the jungle upon the fleet's arrival.

Money in this place varied, and as each day passed the prices raised, but from the start a penny was a penny just like it was in the

Chapter Eleven

States. They didn't mean much unless they came in large quantities. The silver pieces, like the dime and the quarter, made the trade very well the majority of the time. If a sailor shined it the night before while shining your shoes for inspection, he might get a little more out of it; of course, four shiny quarters also went much farther than a dollar in this place also. It seemed that, although school was being taught by the missionaries of the Plymouth Brethren Society, there was unfortunately not enough of it.

The ship was preparing for sea again, and Larry was now assigned the duties of compartment cleaning and smoke watch. These tasks were to be carried out by two men, so Larry and his partner had the bag, but it was a little better for getting in some sleep than down below. The smoke watch had its station on the lookout platform at Sky Control just above the bridge. This watch was to be set at sunrise, and continued through the day until sundown. The purpose of this watch was for the warning and elimination of smoke from the stacks.

The water-tenders below had a periscope to guide them, and this is where the smoke was controlled; to increase efficiency, the phone talker in the operating space was also connected to the smoke watch phones on Sky Control. There were two stacks, the forward stack being controlled by the forward operating space and the after stack by the after operating space. These stacks had a petition separating the sides into port and starboard and it was the smoke watches job to tell them below which side it was on and the color of the smoke. This would help the first class water-tender who was in control of the forced draft blowers. If Larry pressed the button on his phone, and said, "Number two operating space," the phone talker below would reply, "Number two." At this, Larry would relay, "You have black smoke on the starboard side." The phone talker on the phones below would repeat the same words to the man on the blower throttles— usually a first class or chief water-tender. He would then glance at his periscope and correct the matter by opening his throttle to allow more air. He would keep a constant check on the periscope as he opened the throttle, so as not to exceed the proper air pressure and create white smoke.

The Saga of the Lucky Lou

Black smoke from U.S.S. St. Louis

A light brown haze was efficiency smoke, but at times, especially when expecting contact with the enemy, the stack was to be kept clear. Larry thought it would be nice to stand his watches topside and still be in the engineers department, but after two weeks of steadily patrolling the area of Guadalcanal, it became monotonous. Not too monotonous to give up the all-night sleep he was getting, though.

He looked forward to the fresh air every morning, and the hot, bright, sunshine. He also thought it would be nice to take off his shirt and roll up his pant legs to achieve that golden, bronze look, but all clothing was supposed to be kept on—and buttoned up at that.

When one sailor had the smoke watch, the other sailor would be responsible for the cleanliness of the engineer's compartment. If a sailor was a good salesman or could spread a good line, and could make the crew feel sorry for his weary bones, then they might put their next cigarette butt in the can which was within reach.

The smoke watch didn't have the authority to secure when he felt like it, so he had to get permission from the officer of the watch in the engine room. Often, it took time for action on this request to secure the watch, so Larry would find himself sitting, staring at the

Chapter Eleven

stacks, bitching to a seaman nearby.

He had a lot of spare time to reminisce about his civilian days while gazing at the stacks; he would never have believed that his job description would entail determining the color of smoke. After two weeks it had become monotonous, but this was really only the beginning of his long terms at sea.

Sea-duty at this time was very rugged, but Larry figured he was just as well off as he was in port, because the chief in charge of the compartment had now been given the word to scrape off the paint since it was a fire hazard. After he handled the big paint chipper, operated by compressed air, he was very eager to leave port because he hoped that chipping wouldn't be allowed out at sea due to the noises it created, which submarines could intercept.

Larry also had to standby his compartment for inspection immediately after personnel inspection topside. When his division was done being inspected, he would rush down to the entrance of his compartment, and a few minutes later he would be face-to-face with the captain. Larry would snap to attention and say, "Compartment C-402-L ready for inspection, sir!" as he gave the military salute.

All ships in the Navy are divided into three parts: A, B, and C. The forward part was A, the midship was B, and the after part was C. Likewise, all ships have numbered decks; the number "4" denoted that Larry was on the fourth deck. The last number determined whether it was on the port or starboard side; even numbers being port and odd numbers being starboard. In Larry's case, the number two meant that he was on the port side. The letter "L" meant that it was a living compartment. All ships are arranged in this manner and the moment a sailor hears one of these combinations, he should have a good idea where he is.

The ship, leaving port again for patrol duty in the area of Guadalcanal, was handicapped. There was a severe case of dysentery, the result of the sailors eating too many coconuts on the beach. The ship only had six "heads," and now it had to accommodate nearly 1100 men. This required extra "captains' of the head," as they were now in full-scale operation. At this rate, the ship would soon be on its way back to the states for a load of toilet paper.

Larry often wondered why such a place was called "the head," but no matter what it was called, there was no denying the fact that this spot was one of the Navy's greatest institutions, and the very center of its social life. It was the birthplace of scuttlebutt, and the ornate delivery room in which the "captain of the head" functioned as the midwife for the birth of some of the tallest, wildest tales ever visited upon mankind.

It is in the "head," where a timid soul has only to sit and listen in order to learn the facts of life with startling accuracy and realism. It is the spot where the ribald stories of the day are told and heard—and salty tales they sometimes are. In fact, it was said that there was more genuine wit and humor to be heard there in a twenty-four hour period than in the best $5.00 show on Broadway.

The next goal for Admiral Halsey was Solomon's Ladder, which was 30 miles northwest of Russell Islands. Admiral Halsey wanted them very bad, because the good harbors and airstrips would make a good staging point for the advance into New Georgia.

The Russell Islands also flanked the slot, and with a PT base and a radar station, as well as facilities for planes established there, Guadalcanal could be better guarded as the future base of operations. Spearheaded by the Marines of Carlson's Raiders, and protected by Cruiser Division Twelve and destroyers, the Russell Islands were invaded at dawn on February 21, in the midst of a tropical rainstorm.

Instead of an opposing force, the invaders found the welcome mat laid out for them. Apparently when the Japs left Guadalcanal, they had left the Russell Islands also.

A week after the landing, a steady stream of both men and supplies began coming in nightly; by the end of February, there were over 9,000 men in the islands, mostly units of the 43rd Division, the 3rd Marine Raider Battalion, and 35th Construction Battalion, the 10th Marine Defense Battalion, and other Naval base personnel operating under Rear Admiral Turner, Commander of Amphibious Forces in South Pacific.

Preparations were already being pushed forward throughout the eastern Solomon Islands, and facilities were being enlarged at Tulagi and on Guadalcanal. In a few months, airfields were complete on these islands and were very well staffed, with maintenance units attached. Tank farms and underwater fill lines had been

Chapter Eleven

constructed, and were supplied aviation gasoline from tankers of Koli Point. Improvements were made at Tulagi, and Port Purvis, and by now a seaplane base had been developed at Halavo in the Tulagi area. PT boats were also operating from Tulagi Island, as well as at Calvertville on Florida Island, and the Makambo Islands. At Carter City and Turner City on Florida Island, the amphibious forces had grouped together to make the force even stronger.

Orders of the Day

January 25	Arrived at Espirito.
January 28	Underway with Task Force 67. *Enterprise* and *San Diego* got underway also. No dope but plenty of scuttlebutt.
January 30	Met *Washington, North Carolina,* and *Indiana* with four destroyers. Held maneuvers.
January 31	Still south of Guadalcanal. Refueled *Lamson* this morning.
February 1	Task Force 67 arrived at Espirito Santo at 0800. Refueled and got underway again at 1500.
February 2	Espirito was bombed last night. Met *Enterprise, San Diego,* and destroyers. Operating with them.
February 4	Heavy fighting going on, according to "press news." Haven't seen any yet.
February 5	All ships refueled from a tanker today. We refueled at 2130.
February 7	*Enterprise, San Diego,* and destroyers have left. Still operating south of Guadalcanal, waiting with the rest of the forces for the Japs to make a move. They are north of the Solomons.
February 8	Near dusk, we moved close to three battleships.
February 9	Still operating with *North Carolina, Washington, Indiana,* and destroyers; also with *Saratoga, San Juan, Enterprise, San Diego* groups.
February 10	Refueled all destroyers attached to Task Force 67. We refueled *Lamson*.
February 11	Met *Saratoga, San Juan* group at dusk. *Radford* got a sub.
February 12	All ships refueled from a tanker today. *St. Louis* refueled at 1630. *Saratoga* group left.
February 14	The task force arrived in Espirito.
February 15	Task Force 67 underway from Espirito.
February 22	Arrived in Espirito.
February 28	*Helena* got underway.
March 3	Task Force 18, the old Task Force 67 minus *Helena*,

Chapter Eleven

March 6	got underway today. Task Force 12, another cruiser force bombarded Munda and Villa last night. In addition, they sank two light cruisers or heavy destroyers.
March 8	Task Force 18 fueled from *Sabine* today.
March 12	The task force entered Espirito Harbor at daybreak, provisioned ship, and got underway at 1700. Fired night illumination practice at 2000. Have seven destroyers with us. Flag transferred to *Honolulu*.
March 14	Four destroyers have left.

U.S.S. Strong Delivers Mail To Honolulu

March 17	The four that left us have joined us today after successfully bombarding Villa. They were *Nicholas*, *Radford*, *Strong*, and *Taylor*. All ships refueled from a tanker, except for three destroyers who refueled from the cruisers. *St. Louis* fueled the *Chavelier*.
March 18	*Honolulu* (flagship) left us this morning with four destroyers. Her mission is unknown at present.
March 21	Force entered Espirito after firing A.A. practice.
March 22	*Honolulu* and destroyers entered harbor, but no good dope.

The Saga of the Lucky Lou

March 27	*Nashville* got underway.
March 29	The task force got underway and fired 6-inch practice off Espirito. Force is now comprised only of *Honolulu* (flagship), *St. Louis*, and four destroyers. We are going to look for a Jap convoy or bombard if we don't find it.
April 1	Entered Tulagi Harbor and refueled from *Kanawa*. At 1600, we got underway at 23 knots with *Honolulu*, *Nicholas*, *Radford*, *Strong*, and *Taylor*. At 2400, we headed back for Tulagi with no luck.
April 2	Underway with same force, plus two destroyers, with still no luck. Bombardment was scheduled but orders were changed as *St. Louis* got underway.
April 3	Entered Tulagi at 1630 and refueled from tanker. Then anchored in regular berth. At 1545, we were underway for the third straight night to hunt convoys up around Shortland, New Georgia, and Bougainville Islands. Steamed at 25 knots and arrived in Tulagi 0630.
April 4	2400. Headed back to Tulagi because of eighty enemy aircraft over the hunting grounds. Arrived at Tulagi this early morning and anchored as before. At 1015, had regular morning alert which is usually at 1100. The Japs usually attack Guadalcanal right across the channel. Got underway at 1345 with *Honolulu* and six destroyers. Going up the "alley" again to look for the "Tokyo Express."
April 5	No luck again; about-face. At about 0200, *O'Bannon* picked up a surface target on her radar. She ran within 100 yards of it and fired three salvos. It was an empty sub, and as it went down, *O'Bannon* dropped depth charges on it. Had contacted it on previous nights. Two more destroyers were sent back to help pick up survivors, if any, then proceeded into Tulagi to refuel. Then prepared for another run up the alley.
April 6	Headed back at the usual time. Didn't make contact

Chapter Eleven

with the enemy, although a task force was reported to be in the vicinity. The morning was spent in the straits between Malaita and Florida Islands again. *Helena* joined at noon. At 1600, embarked up the alley at 24 knots. At about 2000, while between Russell and Santa Isbel Islands, the Japs attacked Tulagi and Guadal from the air. Got out just in time. Headed back at 2400 with no luck. At 0630, entered the harbor and refueled.

April 7   Underway at 1145 because of expected air attack. A bombardment was planned, but the Japs fouled those plans. *St. Louis* and three destroyers would have hit Munda, and *Honolulu*, *Helena*, and four cans would have bombarded Vella. Went between Savo and Florida instead, then around Indispensible Straits at 24 knots then retired to the east. Japanese never got within range, but bombed Guadalcanal and Tulagi.

U.S.S. Helena - Sister Ship to U.S.S. St. Louis

U.S. fighters sent up 67; 7 were lost. Japanese send over 70 bombers and 48 fighters; 21 bombers and 25 fighters were shot down. Air attacks in this vicinity have been constant.

April 8   Last night *Strong* picked up a sub at 8000 yards on radar and closed in at 1000. Issued depth charges; it was a sure sinking.

April 9   Met *Chenango*, a converted carrier, and its destroyer escort last night. We operated to the northwest, then towards Espirito Santo where we met *Leander*, a New Zealand cruiser, and sister-ship to *Achilles*. *St.*

	Louis left the carrier.
April 10	Entered Espirito harbor at noon, refueled and anchored. USS Kanawa (AO1), the tanker at Tulagi, and her escort USS Aaron Ward (483), were sunk by the Japanese the day *St. Louis* pulled out of Tulagi.
April 15	*Nashville* entered the harbor; Rear Admiral Ainsworth and his flag were transferred from *Honolulu* and *Nashville*.
April 18	Recreation center is located on Aore Island on one side of the channel with baseball diamonds and other facilities; a beach for swimming is located two miles across the island. There is now beer available; it is rationed per ship, per man (sometimes two bottles and sometimes four). A section gets beer once every four days. Sea Bees maintain grounds and landings; assisted by working parties from designated ships.
May 5	Task Force 18 got underway from Espirito Santos. *Helena* is staying in port for repair work. Only four destroyers with *St. Louis*.
May 6	*Taylor* came alongside to receive a 40 mm water jacket. The operation took five minutes. Resumed original speed and steamed across "Iron Bottom Bay," through Skylark Channel. At 1600, headed up the alley at 25 knots. Going to Vella to protect the work of the mine layers. Condition II set at 1600. At 2400, the minelayers began laying mines. Passed them, then at 0130 met them again and retired eastward at 28 knots. At dawn, was between Russell Islands and Santa Isabel Islands. Minelayers were covered in the harbor by *Radford*.
May 7	At 1800 had emergency general quarters due to enemy aircraft. None came near.
May 8	Received notification that the mines laid the night of the 6th had sunk one cruiser and damaged another. Entered Espirito at 1630 and moored alongside a tanker.
May 11	Task Force 18 got underway with 7 destroyers.

Chapter Eleven

May 12	Anchor fouled; captain ordered it lashed to the side. Steamed through "Iron Bottom Bay" through Skylark channel, then separated. *St. Louis, Jenkins,* and *Fletcher* going between Guadalcanal and Savo; the rest of the force between Savo and Tulagi. Traveled up the alley as usual to bombard objectives on the North Side. Steamed west, south of the Russell Islands, past Rendova in the New Georgias.
May 13	Second Bombardment of Munda. *St. Louis, Fletcher,* and *Jenkins.* 0030 started the approach.
0035	Bogie on *St. Louis* talk. Bogie on port bow. None seem to see *St. Louis.*
0100	On the firing course. Flashed over the horizon indicating the other ships firing.
0104	*St. Louis* commences fire. *Fletcher* has already commenced firing. First salvos landed in the water; next round was right on. Spotting plane reports excellent shooting. Minor return fire. *Jenkins* commences to fire.
0120	*St. Louis* ceases fire.
0125	Speed increased toward 30 knots. Port anchor broke loose from its lashings and punched hole in the side, above the water line, but flooded one storeroom and put six inches in the windlassroom.
0730	Met the rest of the force and learned *Nashville* had a casualty; a gun blew up, killing nine men and injuring fourteen. Aside from anchor trouble, *St. Louis* had six guns out of commission and three radars when firing ceased. 975 rounds of 6-inch and 400 rounds of 5-inch were expended.
1236	Emergency general quarters while in Indispensable Straits due to enemy aircraft over Guadal, Tulagi, and the Russell Islands. Many dogfights.
May 14	*Nashville* buried the dead men at sea. Fired A.A. practice. At 1430 entered Espirito Harbor and refueled.
May 18	*Nashville* left for the States.

Chapter Twelve

A Message from the Captain

On this, the Fifth Anniversary of the *St. Louis*, preparations and training are underway for the largest and most far-reaching war operation the *St. Louis* has yet participated in.

This early action and change of scenery, I know you will welcome after the recent long period of relative inactivity. I also know that when the "chips are down," every officer and man will be in there doing his utmost.

A happy anniversary to a splendid ship's company. May we all celebrate the next one in Tokyo.

Captain R. H. Roberts

R.H. Roberts

Chapter Twelve

A Message from the Commander

Today, the *St. Louis* celebrates her Fifth Birthday. Young in age, she is old in experience. That experience has earned a reputation the Japs fully understand and will learn more about shortly, to wit, that of a fighting s—of a b——.

To a fighting ship and the fine group of officers and men afloat who I am certain will insure that the gallant reputation of the *St. Louis* continues, not only a Happy Anniversary but many happy days.

H.M. Briggs

* * * * * * * * * *

On June 3, 1943, Admiral Halsey, in accordance with Joint Chiefs of Staff directives, issued the basic operation plan. On June 30th, simultaneous landings would be made at several points on Rendova Island, and on New Georgia at Viru Harbor, Segi Point, and Wickham Anchorage.

The main thrust against New Georgia was to come from Rendova; troops from there were to move across Roviana Lagoon to land east of Munda and capture the airfield in a quick stroke. This movement was to be covered by preliminary landings on Sasavele and Baraula Islands, which would secure the Onaiavisi entrance to the lagoon. The attack from Rendova was to be accompanied by the seizure of enemy positions in the Bairoko-Enogai area, in order to prevent the Munda garrison from being reinforced from the north.

As soon as Munda and the Bairoko-Enogai were occupied, preparations were to be made to capture Vila-Stanmore on Kolombangara.

There were to be three major task forces: One under Admiral Turner, sub-divided into two parts; the western force to carry out operations in the Rendova-Munda area, and the eastern force to land at Viru, Segis, and Wickham. The second task force, directly under Admiral Halsey, was to cover the broad operation and furnish fire support. The third was the South Pacific Air Force of Vice Admiral Aubrey W. Fitch, whose job was direct air reconnaissance and striking missions, providing air support, and spotting planes.

The Saga of the Lucky Lou

Rear Admiral Marc A. Mitcher, as Commander of Aircraft in the Solomons, had tactical command of aircraft operation from bases in the Solomons.

1) Task Force Tare (Attack Force)- consisted of transports, L.S.T.'s, destroyers, minesweepers, L.C.T.'s, A.P.O.'s, L.C.I.'s, and Russell's M.T.B. Squadron.
2) Task Force Fox (Air Support)- consisted of all South Pacific aircraft, land-based and tender-based, and initially aircraft of Carrier Division 22. The combat planes were 258 fighters, 193 light bombers and 82 heavy bombers, including PB4Y's, whose primary mission was search.
3) Task Force How (Covering Force)- Task Group Abb consisted of Rear Admiral Walden. L. Ainsworth's cruisers—crudin (9), and Captain Francis X. McInerney's destroyers. Task Group Baker consisted of Rear Admiral Aaron S. Merrill's cruisers—crudin (12), minelayers, destroyers. Task Group Charlie consisted of Rear Admiral DeWitt C. Ramsey. Task Unit Victor consisted of carriers, crudin (2), destroyers. Task Unit Williams consisted of Rear Admiral Glenn B. Davis' battleships and destroyers. Task Group Dog consisted of Rear Admiral Harry W. Hill's battleships. Task Group Easy consisted of Rear Admiral Andrew C. McFall's carriers and destroyers. Task Group Fox consisted of Ground Force Reserve Major General Robert S. Beightler and 37th Division, United States Army, less two combat teams.

* * * * * * * * * * *

June 8 Underway with Task Force 18 for gunnery practice. Entered harbor at 1630.
June 15 Number five tug towed in a two-man Jap sub.
June 16 Another alert at midnight as usual. The planes got close, but in the range of *St. Louis* guns.
June 28 Underway at 1330 to support offensive operations in the Solomons. Pit log- 37,985.

Chapter Twelve

June 30 Had a plane casualty. Pilot and radioman were thrown out and later picked up by *O'Bannon*.

July 1 Another plane casualty of the exact same kind as yesterday. The two men were also picked up. Our forces have captured Viru Harbor and Rendova. Lost the transport *McCawley*. 65 out of 110 planes downed.

July 2 Refueled from *Sabine* and got our flyers back. Then the task force headed northwest at 20 knots.

July 3 Pit log- 40,000 miles. Bombardment was scheduled but was cancelled. Entered Tulagi Harbor at 1200 and went to general quarters due to enemy planes over Russell Islands. Underway at 1430 to protect Rendova from bombardment. Three Jap cruisers and four destroyers have been reported in vicinity. Headed west at 24 knots. West of Russell Islands, passed an armada of landing craft, headed for N. Georgia presumably. Reached Rendova at 2230 and slowed to 18 knots for patrol. At about 0200, headed back after no contact with the enemy at 24 knots. Sounded general quarters at 0245 on radar contact, which turned out to be the landing craft, escorted by PT boats returning to Russell. Off Russell at daybreak. Entered Tulagi at 1100, another conference, and then off again at 25 knots to bombard Villa for a landing force. At 2200, *St. Louis* went to general quarters. Forty miles from Kolombangara at 2245.

July 5 Bombardment of Villa by Task Force 18. Cruisers *Honolulu*, *Helena*, *St. Louis*. Destroyers: *Nicholas*, *O'Bannon*, *Chevalier* and *Strong*. 0000- land on Port Hand. 0025- on firing course. 0026- *Honolulu* opens fire. 0028- *St. Louis* opens fire. 0035- large fire on the beach. 0036- troops landing on beach now. 6-inch guns cease fire. 976 rounds. 0040- started firing at opposition. 0045- torpedo passes astern of *St. Louis*. 0050- *Strong* sends out SOS; she is hit by torpedo. 0055- *Strong* is sinking. 0100- two screening destroyers are dropping depth charges. 0115- *O'Bannon* and *Chevalier* meeting strong opposition. 0130- flares and starshells over rescuing destroyers. 0133- *Chevalier's* number three mount blows up. 0140- *Jenkins* going back. 0145- *Strong* has submerged. *Strong's* depth charges can be felt going off. *Chevalier* went alongside *Strong* to take off personnel; as she backed down to leave, a rack of depth charges off *Strong's* fantail rolled in the water, exploding and damaging *Chevalier's* bow. Number six bulkhead is holding though. 0150- shore batteries firing at landing force. *O'Bannon* and *Chevalier* silence them. 0151- searchlight on the horizon. 0155- shore batteries open up at *St. Louis* again but 5-inch kills them. 0157- *Chevalier* firing off port beam at torpedo plane close to *O'Bannon*. 0200- lots of fire on the beach. 0205- mount number three has a jammed powder case. All surrounding and mount personnel have been removed from area. 0210- *Jenkins* ordered to drop back with *O'Bannon* and *Chevalier*, who are coming up on starboard quarter. 0320- *Chevalier* reported rescuing 248 men and 7 officers. 0325- Condition Red set at Russells and Guadalcanal. We are now retiring to the eastward. *Nicholas* met us off the Russells to escort *Chevalier* into Tulagi. We are now headed for Espirito. 1500- Task Force 18 now consisting of *Honolulu*, *Helena*, and *St. Louis* with *O'Bannon* and *Jenkins*, reverse course 180 degrees and head north at 24 knots. We have been ordered to intercept the "Tokyo Express" seen by recon. planes in Shortland Island Harbor, all steamed up. 2145- Pit log at 41,200. 2130- Now at lower end of New Georgia. We are steaming at 28 knots and the P.B.Y. "Blackcats" are accounting for the Japs now.

July 6- 0000- Sounded general quarters. 0145- surface contact 17,000 yards on starboard bow. 0157- *St. Louis* opens fire with 6-inch battery on large target. 0201- cease fire. 0202- shifted targets during lull. 0203- standby to reverse course. 0204- fires on several targets. 0205- *St. Louis* now in lead, *Helena*, then *Honolulu*. 0206- torpedo wake astern. 0207- torpedo wake off starboard bow.

Chapter Twelve

0208- torpedo passed under us about mount number three supposedly. 0209- commence fire. 0210- first salvo direct hit. 0211- one enemy ship blew up. 0212- shifted targets. 0214- cease fire. Stand-by for another run. 0215- target speed is now zero. 0218- *Helena* opened fire off port beam. 0219- thirty rounds of ammunition per turret left. 0220- another enemy blown up. 0221- commence firing. 0222- cease fire. 0223- directors 1 and 2 lost target. They think it sunk. 0224- *Helena* and *Honolulu* still firing, but can't find any more targets. 0229- another target on screen. 0230- Jap ship burning on starboard side. 0232- at 332 degrees relative, surface target at 17,000 yards. 0233- several underwater explosions felt. 0237- 100 rounds of powder left between turrets four and five. 0240- opened fire with star shells at target 12,000 yards away. 0242- one of our destroyers is firing off our starboard bow. 0245- still making 25 knots. Course 242 degrees. 0248- unidentified target at 5,000 yards off starboard beam. 0249- radar out of commission. 0251- Admiral Ainsworth orders cease fire. 0252- heavy underwater explosion felt. 0253- no more targets. 0254- speed now 28 knots, course 290 degrees. 0255- *Helena* dropping back. 0308- heavy underwater explosion felt. 0313- two of our destroyers are being sent into the harbor to look for ships. Can't locate *Helena*. 0319- surface contact on screen, off port bow at 5, 000 yards. 0323- bow of ship has been sighted sticking straight up out of the water. May be *Helena*. 0324- standby to illuminate with searchlights to look for *Helena*. 0326- *Honolulu* is illuminating with lights now. 0327- fifteen miles from Northern new Georgia. 0330- searchlights have picked up an object in the water. Radio report "sorry to report object sighted CL50." 0031- standby for 28 knots. 0332- *Radford* is investigating what is believed to be the wreckage of *Helena*. 0333- it is *Helena's* wreckage. She's believed to have been sunk by torpedoes. 0334- no survivors picked up yet. *Helena* believed to have been sunk when last heavy water

The Saga of the Lucky Lou

explosion was felt. 0335- *Radford* and *Jenkins* standing by to pick up *Helena* survivors. 0337- official report; *Helena* was sunk during action with enemy. 0340- speed now 28.5 knots. 0341- destroyers report they are in midst of survivors. 0345- now retiring to Tulagi at 28 knots. All ships in Jap task force are believed sunk. 0348- target dead ahead. Planes reported five miles astern. 0350- a report from destroyers that they had picked up 400 survivors so far. 0402- *Radford* reports a large ship 13,000 off her bow. 0406- *Radford* is being attacked while picking up survivors. Standby for 180 degree turn to go back and stand by *Radford*. 0411- two large ships coming out of Kula Gulf. 0412- *Nicholas* is still picking up survivors. Both of the enemy ships have opened fire. *Radford* seems to be in trouble. 0415- *Nicholas* has engaged the two ships and is launching a torpedo attack against them. *St. Louis* is closing slowly but still too far away. 0432- enemy ships can't be found so *St. Louis* is once again heading for Tulagi. 0445- all stations rest easy. *Radford* and *Jenkins* still picking up survivors. 0515- report from destroyers, they are finishing off *Helena*. 0642- light ship. 0645- the screening destroyers report: *O'Bannon* has expended all but five torpedoes, and *Nicholas* has expended all. 0700- ninety friendly planes in vicinity. 0730- *Radford* and *Jenkins* report that survivors are scattered and it took some time to get them. 0800- in the last two days, we have expended 175 tons of ammunition, 81,000 gallons of fuel oil, fired 1,100 rounds of shells during battle (6-inch), or forty-three, fifteen, six-inch gun salvos. 0830- twenty enemy planes over Kula Gulf headed this way. 0900- thirty unidentified aircraft picked up. 1027- *Radford* and *Jenkins* coming in. *Jenkins* transfers over 300 survivors to *Honolulu* and *Radford* transfers 438 to *St. Louis*. 1630- underway for Espirito with five destroyers. Pass Task Force 19 which is probably headed for Munda.

Chapter Thirteen

"I am ready to believe the *St. Louis* was lucky," author Duncan Norton-Taylor told the *Hubble Bubble*, recalling the first battle of the Kula Gulf.

"During part of the bombardment when the noise of the six-inch guns had become more than I could bear, I had crossed over to the disengaged side (I was on the bridge) and was standing there staring into the darkness when I saw the wake of a torpedo headed for us on a collision course. I foolishly climbed up on the rail and leaned over to see if indeed the fish was going to hit us. It did! It was a dud—Lucky Lou and I were both lucky that night. I acquired some dubious fame among my fellow correspondents in Noumea as the jackass who climbed up on the railing when, etc. etc."

In a letter to the *Hubble Bubble*, author Duncan Norton-Taylor wrote: "Incidentally, I dubbed the *St. Louis* "The Maiden" in my book. Navy censorship wouldn't let me use her real name. The flag in our three-cruiser force was, as I remember, the *Honolulu*. I had to call her "The Flag." Funny, censors let me call *Helena* by her right name."

Reprinted by Special Permission of the Author
Duncan Norton-Taylor

<u>The Maiden</u>

I felt lighthearted. I looked forward to this assignment as a kind of climax. When the operation was over I intended to return to

Noumea. My office expected me back in New York around the first of August and I wanted to get over to Australia for a look at General Douglas MacArthur's Southwest Pacific command. The cruiser force would probably go south after the bombardment to refuel and this ought to fit into my plans, which were to get air transportation from Noumea to Sydney. By a somewhat circuitous route, I was on my way home.

There were three newsmen on the mission—Allan Jackson, B.J. McQuaid of the Chicago Daily News, and I. A destroyer from the force picked us up at Koli Point. Her officers invited us to stay aboard for the show, but I felt that I would be more secure aboard one of the cruisers, which loomed up impressively in Tulagi Harbor. They ferried us over to the cruiser-flagship in a small boat, and we climbed up an accommodation ladder—I dragging my kitbag—to report to the task force commander.

He was a beefy, sunburned man with the rank of rear admiral. His executive officer told us that we would have to be assigned to separate ships. "We're pretty crowded," he explained. McQuaid cleared his throat and declared that he thought he should stay aboard the flagship since, in addition to the Chicago Daily News, he represented a news syndicate. Allan had spent several weeks on one of the other cruisers, the *Helena*, and would like to go back to her. I got the third cruiser by elimination. Her name cannot be disclosed. But she can more or less appropriately be referred to as The Maiden. She was a virgin among all her tough, scarred sisters who made up the rest of the force; the two other cruisers and four lean destroyers.

Allan and I climbed over the flagship's side again and into a launch. A wind was skipping across the harbor, and when our small boat tried to put on any speed she dipped her nose into the waves and we all got wet. But a lieutenant urged the coxswain to step on it: "We're pulling out of here in a few minutes." We nuzzled alongside The Maiden and I begged for a line which they finally threw me. I tied an end through the grips on my bag, and watched them haul it aboard, and climbed up after it.

Half an hour later The Flag, *Helena*, The Maiden, with four destroyers on their flanks, steamed out of Tulagi Harbor and headed northwest up on the water highway which Pacific veterans call "The

Chapter Thirteen

Slot." It was the Fourth of July.

Our operations plan was simple. Kula Gulf is a funnel with the coast of Kolombangara forming on one side and the coast of New Georgia on the other. We were to enter the funnel, rush along the Kolombangara side, bombard Villa, make a U-turn and plaster Bairoko Harbor and Rice Anchorage on the New Georgia side on the way out. This maneuver was designed to throw the Japs off-balance long enough for a landing force to pour into Rice and establish a beachhead. The greatest danger would be coastal batteries and submarines, with which Kula Gulf was reportedly infested.

Kula Gulf Action

As we steamed past Savo Island, I felt only a tremor of anxiety. The Maiden looked well able to take care of herself. From her long sharp bow to her broad stern, which carried two plane catapults, she bristled with armament. Her main battery in five great turrets consisted of fifteen six-inch guns, capable of throwing out some seven tons of explosives a minute. Eight five-inch rifles, twice as many as the average destroyer's main armament, made up her second battery. Twenty and forty millimeter automatics sprouted lushly like asparagus along the length of her deck and from towers and elevated platforms. For protection, she was girdled with a belt of 6-inch armor.

The Maiden's designation was a "light cruiser." Actually, she was larger than many heavy cruisers. The essential difference was that she mounted lighter guns. The heavies carried eight-inch rifles for their main. She was five times the tonnage of the destroyers bucking along on her flanks. Below decks, where bulkheads were raw and scarred, scraped of paint, she was a honeycomb of passageways and compartments. In her stern was an airplane hangar large enough to accommodate a basketball court.

That afternoon I was more interested in her topsides. I knew from experience that once the night closed down, I would be unable to move around the strange, complex structures of her. I would have to pick some spot and stay there. Captain Colin Campbell referred me to the chief engineer, Commander Graham Gill, and as we plowed up The Slot that sultry afternoon, Gill showed me around. He took me up to Sky Tower Number 2. "I think you could see pretty well from here," he said, leaning out and scowling fore and aft. We tried the bridge. We climbed up on the machine gun platform above it. "Of course no place topside has much protection," he said. I think he had read my thoughts. The only protection on the machine gun platform was a waist-high splinter shield of thin steel. Overhead was nothing but the sky. There was no place above deck safe from plunging shell fire, which might do the ship no vital harm but would play havoc with the personnel. For a panicky moment, I considered staying below but there was no guarantee that I would be safe there either. Torpedoes might breach her. As formidable as she was, The Maiden all at once seemed very naked. She was some 600 feet long with some 60 feet beam, which is a large target. In the end, Gill thought, the machine gun platform would be the best place from which to observe. "I think it will be all right," I said without eagerness. I had the feeling that this was going to be a memorable Fourth of July.

It was still not the fourth back in the States. But by the time we had begun our attack, the east coast of America would be in the middle of the morning of a safe and sane Independence Day. My daughters would probably be getting the sail on their small boat for the holiday races at the yacht club. I hoped that Peg had managed the trip to Oxford all right. It was a long time since I had had any mail. There should be an accumulation for me when I got back to

Chapter Thirteen

Noumea. We steamed in to the gray, curtained, rainy night. I was suddenly, deeply worried about myself.

The cabin they put me in was forward of the wardroom and belonged to Lieutenant Lawrence Gladding Lewis and Ensign James Jarrell Pickle. Pickle had been dispossessed to make room for me. But he assured me that it was all right; he had another place to bunk. We would go to general quarters so no one would be able to hit the sack until daybreak and then—Pickle was resigned to suffering—he would probably have to stand his regular watch. I found out then that The Maiden had been up The Slot the night before, hunting an enemy force somewhere north of Munda. Lewis and Pickle showed some strain. But they were looking forward to the party tonight with grim excitement. They told me to help myself to towels, soap, hair tonic, shaving cream or anything else. A steward brought me a life jacket, an anti-flash burn suit and gloves. I had my own helmet. The head of a Saint Bernard dog pasted on a locker drawer looked at me lugubriously. The caption underneath said: "I will wait." On another door was the picture of a svelte and bosomy lady in undress. Someone had written under the picture: "Right down your alley."

The Maiden's big wardroom was crowded at evening mess. At our table sat Captain Campbell's executive officer, a chesty, fiery-eyed, bull-voiced little man named John Florance. We had turkey; for dessert, ice cream with chocolate sauce. Florance interceded with the stewards to get me a second dish. I seemed to have a large, morbid appetite. We listened to the evening broadcasts from the West Coast. On the day Kelly Turner had moved onto Rendova, General MacArthur's forces had occupied Trobriand and Woodlark Islands, in accordance with the plans. MacArthur's landing had been unopposed. MacArthur was in command of the Southwest Pacific but the broadcast made it appear that he had actually directed the Rendova Landing. The Rendova operation had been Turner's show, and Halsey's. I found out later that MacArthur was no less to blame for the confused reporting of the affair than the news broadcasters and the Navy itself; the Navy refused to release the names of its commanders until many days later.

The Saga of the Lucky Lou

General Douglas MacArthur

Time dragged by. The stewards had cleared the tables and had lashed tables and chairs together. Men coming into the wardroom from the weather deck reported that it was raining. I decided to wear my raincoat—which covered me down to the ankles—instead of the anti-flash suit. It was time finally to get ready. I strapped the inflated, rubber lifebelt around my waist over my long GI raincoat. An officer had lent me a pair of infrared goggles which would guard my eyes from gun glare, he said, and my face from flesh burns. If I wore them for ten or fifteen minutes before going out on deck I would not have to suffer a period of night blindness. I put them on. Several of The Maiden's officers looked me over and assured me that I was properly dressed and equipped. I decided I was ready at last, donned my helmet and went out.

The glasses did not seem to have done much good because I was blind as a bat. I groped through a jungle of stanchions, felt someone brush past me, grabbed him and asked if he was going up on the bridge. A voice said, "Yes, hang on," and I hung onto his arm, stumbling up the inclined ladder after him. I realized then that the red goggles were almost opaque, designed to be worn only as a protection against light and I took them off, feeling a little foolish and

Chapter Thirteen

now able to see quite well. It was a black night, filled with a fine sifting rain. Unescorted, I climbed up the ladder to the machine gun platform.

The gunners, dressed in bulky, protective clothing, lounged at their stations. They were not expected to take part in the bombardment. They were standing by in case of air attack. I could just make out the snouts of their pom poms vaguely silhouetted against the sky. In the center of the platform was the cool, steel mass of the fire control tower, which I felt my way around.

I held onto the shield, with the warm wind in my face. The other ships in our force were invisible. Occasionally, the gunners muttered among themselves or a talker passed a routine order in a flat, mechanical voice. There was no other sound but the rush of our wake. I began to wonder what I was doing here.

I thought I could see a dim shoreline on our starboard side. I was very sure of it. I knew then that we must have changed our course, that the shoreline was the coast of Kolobangara, that we must be turning into the funnel. It was fifteen minutes past midnight by the illuminated dial of my wristwatch. I stuffed cotton into my ears, put the red goggles on and settled my helmet firmly. I remembered the advice a Marine had given me not to buckle the strap. "Leave it loose. If a shell fragment hits your hat and the strap is buckled under your chin, you might get your neck broke."

In a moment now we would start bombarding. I think I worried about that more than anything, even more than the enemy's reaction.

We had some warning on The Maiden. Ahead of us, the shape of a ship leaped into sight, silhouetted against a great cloud of fiery smoke. The Flag had just opened up and the *Helena*, next in line, was limned in the glow which looked pink through my goggles. Pink were the small, bright globes which popped out singly and in clusters and floated toward Kolombangara's bank, a sleeping shore. Distant thunder began rolling back across the water. Sixty seconds— then the *Helena's* shape dissolved in the flash of her own guns and the thunder grew in volume. Bright globes—tracer shells—multiplied and soared across the sky. In photographs, the tracers showed as streaks. It is a falsification of the camera. They look more like Christmas tree balls and it is possible to follow them with the eye, until they reach the end of their trajectory, where they simply vanish in the pockets of the darkness with no apparent effect. It is incredible how pretty and harmless they look. It was our turn now. My face was stiff. I hung unto the shield, glancing in the direction of our forward turrets, gaping in the direction of the coast.

The Maiden suddenly hissed. I learned later that it was the noise of compressed air being blown through her guns to clean out the gasses, but I did not know it then and I almost jumped out of my raincoat. I hardly had time to recover from the surprise of it when we exploded.

Even through the protective goggles, the glare of her six-inch guns was like a blow. I instinctively ducked. Sight and sound were merged into one physical concussion that sent me staggering backwards. I was shocked and terrified and angry. The platform seemed to rise under me. I wanted to yell a protest. Possibly I did. No one could have heard me, not even myself. Clouds of smoke filled with fiery particles swept back toward me and I crouched behind the shield. There was a strange, familiar odor which, when I grew accustomed to it, I tried to identify but could not. There was silence after the detonation, space for me to suck in my breath. I tried to recover myself. But there was no time. The Maiden exploded again. We were firing salvos, all fifteen of our six-inch guns simultaneously letting loose. Intervals between were in seconds. I put my fingers up under my helmet and pressed my ears. The cotton plugs were not enough. I leaned my back against the fire control tower, stumbled forward again across the platform, let go of my ears and hung onto the shield. The men around me, the pom pom gunners, kept jumping into view like erratic figures in a broken movie film. Their shoulders were hunched, their heads down—then they would vanish, to reappear, to vanish again. I had only one sensation; passionate longing for it all to cease. But it kept on and on, in an interminable delirium. Then there was silence at last, which stretched out. Momentarily it was over.

I learned later that those first salvos had lasted only ten minutes. I learned that at one point an observer in a Catalina somewhere above us reported by radio: "There's a fire on the beach, probably an ammunition dump." But from where I stood I could see nothing.

Chapter Thirteen

I pulled the goggles off and stared into the darkness, thinking that after all that violence something must be happening somewhere. But for all I could see Kolombangara was the same blank, sleeping shore.

We changed course then, making the U-turn. The night was split open again by fire, and the uproar engulfed us. The Maiden's secondary battery of five-inch guns was bellowing. Not as loud, they were sharper, more violent. In the midst of their dreadful slamming I heard an occasional sharp squeal of a shell whipping across the sky.

The Maiden was quiet now. She was fleeing through the flat, dark sea toward the open end of the funnel. I seized the moment to climb down the ladder to the bridge below. It was apparent that the men on the bridge were anxious to get out of the Gulf. Sooner or later, the enemy would recover from his surprise and react. Suddenly he did. We were bathed in a soft light. It must have been a flare dropped by a Jap float plane somewhere above us. The gun crews yelled. A signalman shouted: "Now they're coming, now we'll get it." But they never did come. We rushed through the area of sinister light while the ack-ack gunners on the decks below stood with their heads back and their faces to the sky, until we had buried ourselves in the darkness again.

On the bridge there was the constant, crowded movement of men, the buzz of orders given and acknowledged, the sound of voices on our TBS as the task force commander directed our movements through the blind night. "Paul from Peter—we have an unidentified surface contact..." "Peter from Paul, I think it is one of our ships..." Then abruptly a sharp voice said without formality: "Hurry—come quick!"

The bridge became an agitated area of dimly discerned, talking men. A figure beside me crouched behind a range finder. Some of them thought the cry was a trick. It was possible that a Jap ship somewhere along the coast was trying to disorganize us, send us groping around the harbor looking for one of our units supposedly in distress in order to give their torpedo bombers time to get up off Villa airfield.

But the plea was authentic. All at once, not far off, on our starboard hand, a cloud of fire and smoke bubbled out, lighted up the unmistakable, rakish shape of an American destroyer. Messages crackled over TBS. It was the destroyer *Strong*. She had been torpedoed. Another can was already picking up survivors.

Our sound gear verified the presence of enemy subs. The big ships had to get out of the funnel. The burning *Strong* was too far away for us to see any of the details of her distress—men rushing about her decks abandoning her and jumping into the Gulf. Her fire flared up to reveal the sharp bow of another vessel, evidently the destroyer which had gone to her aid. Then the flames seemed to die out. The stricken ship was far astern of us now and gradually vanishing. A voice said she was sinking in 100 fathoms of water. I admired the speaker's attention to detail.

As for us, we were crawling warily out of the funnel. The rescue work and other secondary chores would be left to the cans. The landing force had come in, meanwhile, and off in the darkness was pouring onto the New Georgia coast. We could see nothing of this until, from the beach which we had shelled a good distance astern of us, little bright Christmas tree balls began to loop. A Jap land battery which had survived our bombardment was trying to defend Rice Anchorage. We heard one of our landing force ask for help, he couldn't get in the face of the fire, he said.

One of our busy destroyers said shortly, "I'll get the son-of-a-bitch," and from a point out in the Gulf pea-sized lights began to flow toward the enemy battery so that for a few minutes the exchange of fire looked like some kind of Times Square sign. I heard the distant banging of their guns. And then the lights ceased to pop from the enemy shore.

Two destroyers which had gone to the aid of the *Strong's* men reported that they were under torpedo plane attack. I think they were reporting this just as a matter of general interest. The action was taking place miles away from us now. They said they were using ack-ack. We were concerned but we were not waiting around to see the results. The cans announced that they had beaten off the attack. Now they were also heading out of the harbor, they said. Hardly ninety minutes had elapsed since we had opened up. Our whole task force, minus the *Strong*, retired from Kula Gulf.

I felt a kind of incredibility, now that it was over. Never had

Chapter Thirteen

there been any sense of contact with the enemy. We had gone in, had blasted away and rushed out and the only evidence of the Jap's presence had been the *Strong*, smoking and sinking, and the one shore battery briefly lobbing shells into the darkness.

Even those had been remote incidents, seemingly of no great consequence. Standing all the time on the edge of catastrophe, you cannot do any more than make a note of the catastrophe overtaking others. You are too far away to see them actually dying in the water. You have nothing but a few seconds' glimpse of their ship on fire and then it has vanished. You have room for very little of any emotions outside of relief over your own escape.

We steamed at full speed down the New Georgia coast. Before daylight we wanted to be well away from the vicinity of Munda airfield. I stayed on the bridge with my arms hanging over the windscreen, occasionally dropping into a half-sleep. I would have sat on the deck but I was afraid of getting stepped on. The night exhaustedly dragged itself out and dawn lightened the east. Still figures of men standing or sitting at their stations began to emerge. The signs of the violence which we had been through were the empty shell cases strewn on our decks and the dark blotches on the barrels of our guns left by the terrible heat. The other ships in our force became visible, shaking out the white petticoats of their wakes. The morning was gray and blank. On our starboard at last were the friendly Russells.

The wardroom had a good smell of coffee and bacon and cigarettes. We sat around the long tables and reviewed the night's operation. A big, red-headed lieutenant came in, sat down and rubbed his hands over his grapefruit. I asked him how he had enjoyed the night's business and he said, "It was all right but it doesn't take the place of a woman." He said I could quote him. Gradually, the strained look vanished from men's faces. The starboard watch had to go on and they went out griping about their lousy luck because some of them had only two or three hours sleep in the last twenty-four.

I finally shuffled into my cabin. I was glad that I had been through the action but I could not say that I had enjoyed it. I was happy that it was over. I packed some of my things in my kit bag. With luck, I might be in Noumea the following night. I stared at myself in the mirror and considered shaving but decided to hell with it and crawled up into Pickle's berth and stretched out. The blower roared dully and the small sounds of the ship under way began to repeat themselves. Footsteps padded along the passageway. We must have been running through the smooth water off Guadalcanal because now there was not the faintest motion. I had a vast sense of relief and security.

About four o'clock in the afternoon I awoke. Groggy from sleep and the heat, I wrapped myself in a towel and tramped through the wardroom to the showers. An officer was balancing on one leg and carefully drying his toes. Conversationally, I asked him when he thought we would get to Espirito. He put his foot down. "Espirito?" he said. "Where have you been?"

"Asleep."

"Since about 1500, we've been heading back for Kula Gulf."

Lieutenant (j.g.) Bill Hewitt, an ex-advertising copy writer from San Francisco, told me later that when he had gone on the inter-ship phone to pass the word to the machine gun stations that we were making a 180 degree turn and were going back to the Gulf, there was a dead silence. That morning coming out of Kula, when Hewitt had told them that we were retiring, they had piped up: "We really knocked the hell out of 'em, we sure threw it at 'em, sir. How'd you like that, sir?" Now, Hewitt said, he had to keep hollering at them to acknowledge until they finally gulped, "Aye, aye, sir." I knew just how they felt.

We had been ordered back to engage an enemy naval force which was supposed to be coming down from the Shortlands. The Japs were going to try to land reinforcements on Munda. They were headed in that direction. Our reconnaissance planes had reported that they were in considerable strength. We hoped to arrive in Kula Gulf in time to intercept them.

Captain Campbell made a speech. Campbell was a small, soft-spoken man but his voice was loudly amplified over the ship's public address system. He told the crew: "The Tokyo Express is heading south and we hope to engage and destroy it." An uncertain cheer went up from The Maiden's deck, where the men stood listening with sober expressions.

I felt strange and frightened and remote. I had moments of

Chapter Thirteen

resentment against the Japs. I had moments of desperate hope that something would intervene, that we would get a message that the enemy force had turned tail, for instance. No such message ever came. The hours of daylight flew past, and at full speed we galloped back. I unpacked the gear that I would need. Sometime after midnight on another black, rain-wet night, we plowed once again around the head of New Georgia.

I had stationed myself on the navigating bridge within listening range of the TBS with my stomach in knots. The startling part of our contact with the enemy was its suddenness. At 1:30, we were proceeding across the top of the Kula Gulf. I had no hint of the enemy's presence. The talk over TBS was blurred and mostly in code which made no sense to me. Then I heard a voice: "Prepare to engage..." To engage what, I could not tell. The Maiden's guns hissed. "Stand by to fire..." There was orderly, dark confusion in the crowded wheelhouse. Where I stood on the port wing of the bridge, men held their ears and waited. Several officers watched fixedly through night glasses. One talked, stood as immobile as a statue, one hand at an earphone, the other at his mouthpiece. Then, once more the dreadful detonation of the main battery struck like a giant fist and I staggered drunkenly around, freshly appalled. Occasionally, I was conscious that I was shriveling up inside my coat, elbows pressing into my sides, head down, knees bent. I straightened up, presently found myself in the same curious, quaking position again. An officer went past me with his hands at his side, bowed like a man walking against a great wind.

Instead of the red goggles, I wore clear anti-flash glasses so that I would be able to see a little into the darkness. But as much as a glance at the muzzles of our guns left me blinded. The clouds of fire swept over us and I smelled and recognized that odor now. It was the minstrel-show smell of burnt cork-wadding shot from the powder cases. In an interval of quiet when we checked our fire, a voice said: "Shift targets."

So far as I could tell, our arching tracers had simply disappeared without effect into the night. There had been no reaction from the enemy. I learned later that we had made contact with three, possibly four cruisers, and five destroyers as they were running along the Kolombangara coast, headed out. They had already landed their troops on Munda and were making tracks for home. We had come across the top of the Gulf and in a line to intercept them, had plotted their course and speed and had opened up on them before they even suspected our presence. Before they could recover from their enormous surprise, we were drenching them with steel.

I stared ahead at our fulminating sisters. The Flag leaped into sight, vanished, leaped into sight again, vanished in the spaced bursts of her salvos. But the Helena was continuously visible, wreathed in smoke, spurting a solid sheet of white flame while traces flowed out of her in streams. She seemed to be out of position but I thought nothing of it then. Our forward guns had exploded into action again and I caught the full glare of them and recoiled, ducking blindly across the after part of the bridge to the darkness on the starboard side. I was holding to the rail when I saw the torpedo wake.

It was a thick white finger coming straight at us like a chalk line drawn across a blackboard. On this disengaged side of the bridge there was only one other man at the moment—a signalman who screamed: "Torpedo! Torpedo!" But even if anyone had heard him it was too late for The Maiden to dodge. My eyes were fixed on the advancing track. The signalman disappeared from beside me. I thought that The Maiden's speed might yet carry her clear of the converging white finger. I was fascinated and leaned out over the rail to watch and saw the wake end abruptly and squarely against The Maiden's side, amidships.

Men in the engine room, and in repair parties below deck, and in sick bay, and central station, and the control room, and in the magazines and handling rooms under dogged-down hatches, heard it bump and grate along The Maiden's bottom and thought their time had come. They told me afterward that I should have thrown myself flat on the deck to escape flying fragments and the possibility of being flung overboard by the concussion. It was then, thinking back, that I felt a little sick and thankful for some Jap's error of workmanship or calculation. The torpedo was a dud.

At the time, I had no sense of miraculous escape. I did not even think much about the origin of that torpedo, which must have been fired by a submarine since we had no surface contacts on that side of us. I dismissed it and staggered back to our engaged side.

Chapter Thirteen

I was a little more concerned all at once with a sound like a steel rod being whipped through the air. In the gray waves a hundred yards away and lighted by our own unholy glare, geysers shot up. We were under enemy shellfire. It occurred to me that I would be safer on the other bridge but I made no move to retreat there. I was beyond fear now. I could see what looked to be, at the distance, small innocent bonfire burning along the coast of Kolombangara. They were Jap ships which we had kindled somehow with our guns. There was nothing spectacular about them. One fire abruptly went out. Another appeared to fly apart as though someone had kicked a pile of burning leaves. Then it disappeared. It was unbelievable, but these were ships the size of The Maiden herself, exploding into flames and bursting apart.

We changed our course, obedient to the unhurried radio commands from The Flag. "Execute, execute..." Our force had destroyed five ships. We had momentarily lost contact with the others. The survivors, evidently disorganized by the suddenness of our onslaught, had turned and were fleeing back into the funnel of Kula. We turned and must have roughly paralleled their flight. Only a little more than thirty minutes had elapsed since we first opened fire. Then we began slapping away again, this time broad off our starboard beam.

Someone on the bridge said: "Where's The Flag?" For a moment, I remembered the stories I had heard of the Battle of Savo Island, and I felt panic-stricken at the thought of what might happen in the sixteen-mile-wide mouth of the Gulf if we began milling around blindly, firing at each other. But someone said, "I've got her, sir," and gave The Flag's bearing. Through all the complicated turning and wheeling that night, we never lost our station.

Once again, we checked our fire. In the chart house, a talker was repeating: "One definite target." There was a jumble of sound. I heard him give the range and the bearing: "Three-two-two." Then: "Unload guns." The Maiden belched, then the night was still. Then there was no more targets. The Japs had either fled or been erased completely from the dark, wet world.

But the Admiral on the Flag continued to look. "Illuminate to port with star shells, range one-two-four-oh-oh, bearing two-zero-zero." Our after guns spoke and lifted the veil of night astern of us.

The Saga of the Lucky Lou

There was nothing there but the black sea.

Again and again over TBS came the unemotional voice. The Flag had an unidentified target now at 5000 yards, 80 degrees relatives. A destroyer was investigating. The men in The Maiden's control room reported hearing three heavy vibrations; fifteen minutes later reported a series of explosions. Our four destroyers were ordered to search the Gulf for "the bastards." Time ticked by. I had little idea what was going on, except that now we had straightened out in our course and seemed to be gathering speed. I prayed that we were going home. TBS said: "I smell a skunk." An unidentified target. A destroyer was ordered to illuminate. I sensed all of a sudden that there was something amiss.

On our port hand a beam of light shot across the night, falling upon what might have been the conning tower of a submarine. It was gray and dead and derelict in the rolling sea. The Flag asked impatiently: "Who is it? Who is it? Acknowledge." The destroyer said at last: "I am sorry to report, sir, it is Five Zero."

It was the up-ended bow of a ship, not the conning tower of a submarine. It was floating there silently for us to see, the only part of her by which she could be identified. Number 50 was the *Helena*.

TBS was silent. Presently, the destroyer said that she could see survivors clinging to rafts. Another destroyer was also standing by. The Admiral gave his orders to the rest of us. He had to pull out what was left of his investment. The Flag and The Maiden and the two other destroyers would retire. I thought of Jackson, who had asked specifically to be assigned to the *Helena*. We stood out to sea, leaving the two cans behind. The cans always got the dirty work.

We had been on our course for home about twenty minutes, with TBS muttering and chattering, when a voice said: "Large ship closing in on us." I learned later that it was the voice of Captain Francis X. McInerney, commander of our destroyer squadron, who was aboard one of the cans we had left behind. "What shall we do?" McInerney asked calmly. There was a silence. I could imagine the hurried decisions being made aboard The Flag. The Admiral finally said, "Engage the enemy. We are returning to aid you." The Maiden careened in a sharp turn and a talker beside me said, "Oh God!"

Chapter Thirteen

Captain Francis X. McInerney

LCDR Andrew G. Hill

The Saga of the Lucky Lou

Captain Romoser

For McInerney's two cans, the night had only begun when we had started to withdraw. I can only retell their story second hand. We in the main force were miles away in the black morning, with our bellies full of fighting, while their battle was going on. I got the story the next day from McInerney and one of his skippers, Commander William K. Romoser. It began with the torpedoing of the *Helena*.

The big cruiser had been sunk, unknown to us, in the first few minutes of the onslaught. Captain John Cecil had got on a target with his first salvo, had poured out shells like water from a hose, and had already shifted to his third target when his ship ran into torpedo spreads.

The enemy had evidently concentrated on the *Helena*, lighted as she was from stem to stem with fire from her main battery. In the few minutes she was engaged, she fired more than 1000 rounds. Enemy destroyers had begun desperately circling her to get her into torpedo range. The *Helena* closed with them and had brought them under fire with her ack-ack batteries when the first torpedo breached her. Although she was mortally hurt then, she continued to blaze away until two more fish pierced her amidships. She began to break in two. Cecil had no choice but to order her abandoned. He himself

Chapter Thirteen

finally went over the side, into the oil-covered water and just managed to get a handhold on a crowded life raft. He and his men paddled frantically away.

Oil from the *Helena's* shattered compartments had spewed as high as the bridge, but miraculously there had been no great outbreak of fire. She had floated there blackly, her back broken, her tall stacks awry, her ponderous-looking superstructure leaning, her hot guns silent and pointed to the sky. Then her 10,000 tons settled, her stern upended, and with a mournful, vast shushing, with an awesome grinding and protesting, she disappeared, spreading her black oil on the waves.

U.S.S. Helena

The dismembered portion of her bow, with men trapped at their stations inside, had stayed afloat for some time. Then, it too disappeared. Covered with the black blood of her, the survivors paddled despairingly around in the empty sea.

Romoser's ship had found the bow. With his searchlight laying a long shaft across the sea, Romoser had edged carefully into the area where men were flapping their arms and yelling at him. "In the white light, they looked like a school of black fish thrashing around in phosphorescence. They gave us a cheer, and I ordered two boats lowered and they began swimming into them. Many of them had knives in their teeth. They were not certain of our identity and they were prepared to fight for their lives if my ship had turned out to be a Jap."

Romoser had scarcely begun fishing them out when he detected enemy vessels coming out of the Gulf. They were evidently survivors of the main engagement who had scuttled off and now, figuring that they had our destroyers at a disadvantage, were rushing out to fight. McInerney, on the other destroyer, ordered Romoser to break off and attack and Romoser shouted at the *Helena's* men: "Take it easy, we'll be back." The two cans swept off into the darkness to engage the enemy, who had begun firing torpedoes. But the Japs evidently lost their courage and ducked back again into the Kula funnel. McInerney told Romoser to return to the *Helena's* men. The ship McInerney was on, commanded by Lieutenant Commander Andrew J. Hill, would defend him.

Romoser hustled back and fished some 300 more of the *Helena's* hurt, haggard, and thankful men out of the ocean. Then the enemy came out again. McInerney made out at least one of their ships as a large one. It might have been the better part of valor to retire but instead he advised The Flag of the situation.

That was when the Admiral told him to engage and ordered us all back to their assistance.

Romoser, meanwhile, had rushed to Hill's assistance and the two destroyers found themselves in a stalking match. The water around them was streaked with torpedoes and they discharged nine of their own.

There was a sudden detonation, followed by a second one. Romoser opened fire, pouring five-inch shells into the darkness. Hill illuminated with star shells, and there in the smoke of her burning guts was a big Japanese cruiser and, astern of her, a destroyer at which Romoser and Hill slugged away with their main guns. The cruiser had ceased to react. She was dead and sinking. So was the destroyer. There was a third ship but she fled again. McInerney reported to the Flag: "We have no more targets."

We heard that message on The Maiden and turned thankfully homeward again. The curtain of darkness was beginning to lift along the enemy coast of New Georgia.

Romoser and Hill went back to the *Helena's* cheering men. "One

Chapter Thirteen

crowd around a craft was singing 'Happy Days Are Here Again'," McInerney told me. Romoser and Hill put over more whaleboats and slimy, weary men hauled each other out of the sea. The boats carried them to the destroyers.

From the Kolombangara coast the last, nervous Jap once more felt her way. Romoser and Hill broke off to attack again. In the lightening morning they hurled their shells across the sky. The Jap was a destroyer. They poured shells into her with their sharp, yammering five-inch guns. Smoke began to swirl from her and float into the dawn, marking the end at last of the Tokyo Express. Our force had accounted for five Japanese destroyers; three, possibly four, big cruisers. McInerney with his Tin Can Fleet of two stood triumphant in the somber Gulf.

But the sun was coming up over the rim of the Pacific. A lookout reported a submarine periscope. In the sky above Villa airfield, at the far end of the funnel, planes were beginning to circle like roused hornets from their nest. McInerney had to decide then whether to stay and try to recover the rest of the *Helena's* men, or get out before he was attacked from the air. If he stayed, he jeopardized his ships and the survivors they had already taken aboard. He decided to retire.

The Captains left their boats with some of their own crews. Among the men they had to abandon was Cecil, who several times had refused to be taken aboard while men around him were still waiting to be rescued. The stubborn and courageous Cecil had remained in the water the whole time, clinging to the edge of a packed raft.

McInerney's cans turned tail. It must have been an agonizing sight for the *Helena's* unlucky men who were left. But there can be no doubt of the wisdom and necessity of McInerney's choice. His two ships, in the full light of day and jammed with men, steamed at full speed down the New Georgia coast.

The main part of our force crawled into Tulagi Harbor in the middle of a sunny morning. Clouds piled up whitely, roosting on the black shoulders of the mountains. Men on ships at anchor surveyed us curiously. We dropped our hooks. Our two cruisers, we were told, would take over the *Helena's* survivors from the two overloaded cans, which were somewhere astern of us.

St. Louis at Tulagi

Looking like a couple of Hudson River excursion boats, McInerney's two filthy little heroines finally poked their noses into the anchorage. The men on The Flag gave Hill's ship a cheer as she nosed in toward them. Our men were silent at the approach of Romoser's ship. We lined The Maiden's rail, gazing down solemnly on decks piled with empty shell cases, jammed with human cargo. Superstructure, torpedo tubes, gun turrets, decks were smeared with oil from the contact of bodies. Even Romoser's officers and crew were befouled. Most of *Helena's* men had scrubbed the oil from their faces. But their eyes were red and inflamed, their hair black and greasy. Some were half naked. They looked tragic and numbed. They must have known we were searching among them for friends and they watched our faces with a kind of ironic interest.

I looked for Jackson. I heard someone call my name and saw Jackson Allan on the destroyer's bridge taking pictures.

The silent men came aboard over a gangway between our ships. A few had to be supported. There were half a dozen still figures in stretchers who were lifted carefully aboard and taken aft to our sick bay. We gave the *Helena's* heroes ice cream. The stewards doled it out in cardboard cartons, chocolate and vanilla, and they stood around our decks spooning it into their raw faces.

Chapter Thirteen

Jackson had thrown all his clothing away and had borrowed the khakis he was wearing, even the camera he was using. He had lost everything. He had put his camera, money, identification papers, and rolls of film in a ballistic balloon which he carried for just such an emergency. But while grabbing for a raft he had lost the balloon. He had floated in the water a good hour, shaken by concussions, watching tracers soar across the sky over him.

He was going back to Guadalcanal, he said. He asked me to give his wife a ring when I got back to San Francisco and tell her that he was all right and climbed shakily down into a boat which had come alongside and was going across the strait with some officers. B.J. McQuaid also left us at Tulagi, in a hurry to file a story on "the most devastating, the most one-sidedly murderous night sea battle of the Pacific War. Only by a series of fortunate movies did I become the only newspaper writer to participate."

That afternoon our task force sailed south. There was no question now of our returning for another engagement. Our fuel was low and our ammunition was dangerously depleted. Sky and ocean were bright and peaceful. We sat around and listened to the *Helena's* survivors tell their stories. There were morose and dejected men. Their ship had had an awesome record in the Pacific War. In the Battle of Cape Esperance, the year before, the *Helena* had sunk a destroyer and a cruiser, and had helped to sink two other ships of the Jap force. During the whole long, sanguinary Guadalcanal campaign she had been in the thick of it. She had cruised the Solomans area, pounding the Jap shore installations. In the battle of November 12-13, when the *San Francisco* had her bridge blown off, the *Helena* knocked out a Jap cruiser, sank two destroyers, sank the cruiser which had hit the *San Francisco*, and pounded three other enemy ships into pell-mell retreat.

That afternoon we paid her a minor tribute. We stood at respectful attention while a bosun's pipe shrilled aboard The Maiden. Aboard The Flag they were holding services for one of the *Helena's* crew, Fireman I. L. Edwards, who had been in the forward fireroom. Badly burned, he had been carried out by two shipmates and had survived the night on a raft in Kula Gulf. But that afternoon he had succumbed. They sewed him in a bag and somewhere off San Cristolbal consigned his body to the sea.

I went down to my cabin. The sad eyes of the Saint Bernard followed me around. The half-clad lady swung back and forth on an unsecured locker door. I closed and secured it. Pickle was asleep on the upper berth, flat on his back, his two feet in black socks sticking up like sails. Lewis came in and explained: "Pickle had to give up his other sack to one of the survivors. You can take up my berth if you want to. I've got to go on watch." I asked him when we expected to get to Espirito. "Probably not before morning," he said. "But you ought to stick with us. We'll show you some more action."

"That's what I'm afraid of."

"Well, you're lucky to be going home," he laughed. "Some day I'll see you in Richmond, Virginia, again—if I'm lucky."

July 7   At 0830, 78 more survivors were picked up on east side of Kula Gulf; also *Radford* and *Jenkins'* whaleboat crews.

July 8   Task Force 18 arrived in port at 0800 and received quite a hand. Diving inspection proves two or three dents in hull from torpedoes which never exploded.

July 9   Relaxed on Aore Island with beer and Artie Shaw's Navy band.

July 10   Task Force 18 underway early.

July 11   Passed through Skylark channel at about 1630 and was joined by *Leander*. As we went between Savo and Tulagi or Florida Island, headed up the slot, Task Force 19 went between Savo and Guadalcanal headed toward Rendova on the Munda side. Still looking for Japs. Task Force 19 will bombard Munda. 2320- starshells on port bow. 2335- flare on port beam. 2339- flashes of gunfire can be seen on the other side of New Georgia. 2342- two planes,

Chapter Thirteen

Australian Cruiser - Leander

sixteen miles away. 2343- target on horizon 060 degrees. 2357- main battery trained to starboard on probably air target.

July 12 0015- enemy plane approaching again. 0026- mount number four on a single plane. 0040- destroyer on starboard quarter signaling. Lots of Bogies. 0042- another target at 16,000 yards. Our transports entering Kula Gulf. 0048- 290 degrees, one plane. Four lights blinking low on the water. 0055- sky control on plane at 20 degrees. 0110- two floating lights close by. 0130- reversed course. Now in vicinity of Kula Gulf battle. Will patrol and wait here until 0300. 0300- we are now retiring toward Tulagi. Task Force 19 is now bombarding Munda airfield. 0330- little more gunfire across island. 1130- anchored and refueled in Tulagi. 1710- underway, up the alley again. We are going to see if we can meet the Japs tonight. 1945- set Condition II. 1955- Condition Red over Russell Island. 2000- Russell Island under air attack; witnessed the 5" A.A. fire, the ack-ack, and dogfight. Tracer fire and 5" bursts are the only thing visible now. A plane went down in flames.

July 13 Task Force 18 composed of *Honolulu, St. Louis* and *Leander*; destroyers *O'Bannon, Nicholas, Radford, Jenkins, Taylor, Woodworth, Gwin, Farenholt, Maury, Buchanan* and *Ralph Talbot*. 0042- surface contact of six ships at

The Saga of the Lucky Lou

40,000 yards. One cruiser, five destroyers. 0102- radar date: range 22,000, speed 26 knots. 0105- enemy ships now in sight off port bow. 0106- range on four stack cruiser 20,000 yards at 030 degrees. 0109- our destroyers are now launching a torpedo attack. 0111- opened fire to starboard. Enemy cruiser returning fire and using searchlights. 0113- enemy searchlight knocked out. 0114- enemy ship exploded. Several fire on Nip ships. 0115- ship on fire off starboard bow. 0117- heavy explosion underwater felt. 0118- reverse course 180 degrees. One more target left at 10,000 yards on 000 degrees. 0120- opened fire to port. Enemy ship returning fire. 0122- target range 12,000 yards. 0123- heavy underwater explosion felt. 0124- target speed one and a half knots. 0125- *Honolulu* has shifted to rapid fire. 0127- all radars out of commission. 0128- number 1, radar back again. 0129- cease fire. 0134- *Leander* has received torpedo hit forward. Destroyers standing by. 0138- Radar II back in commission. 0140- our course 000 degrees, 27 knots. 0141- our destroyers illuminating the remaining Jap ship. 0145- enemy still firing back. Target speed zero. 0147- *Leander* seems to be dead in water. 0149- three targets (bearing 310 degrees relative) 11,000 yards. 0150- *Leander* reports being able to make 10 knots. 0155- very heavy underwater explosion and jar felt. 0156- torpedo hit up forward. 0159- *Honolulu* opens fire off port bow. Has torpedo hit also. 0209- torpedo hit frame II. 0212- torpedo wake off starboard quarters. 0223- speed 7 knots. 0324- surface target on the screen bearing 315 degrees relative, range 9,000 yards. 0328- air contact 7 miles bearing 175 degrees. 0400- report from bridge that all three cruisers have been hit and destroyers *Gwin* and *Buchanan* have been damaged. *Ralph Talbot* towing *Gwin*. 0435- tug being sent for *Leander*. 0525- arrive in Tulagi about 1600 at this speed. Top speed 16 knots. 0538- unidentified planes closing in. 0600- reports say that we sank all targets, one four-stacked cruiser and five destroyers. 0604- planes coming in at 295 degrees. 0615- nine groups of our

Chapter Thirteen

planes reported about forty miles from here. 0700- several pieces of the torpedo have been found on the ship. One weighs about forty pounds. 0715- set Condition II. *Leander* and destroyers out of sight. 1500- observed Task Force 19 headed toward New Georgia. 1600- moored to piling along the beach in Tulagi Harbor.

St. Louis bow damage, buckled plates, being repaired at Tulagi

July 14 Underway for Espirito at 0600. Pit log: 43,740. Speed almost 13 knots. Destroyers are *Woodworth, Farenholt, Ralph Talbot,* and *Buchanan.* Had air and sub emergency. Might have gotten sub.

July 16 Arrived in Espirito Santo and moored alongside *Vestal.* Unloaded fuel and ammunition. Pit log: 44,395. Ship damaged back to frame number 23. *Vestal* will do repair work as far as practicable as the new dry dock is not ready. Bow welded closed.

July 28 Captain Colin Campbell received the Navy Cross (for the first battle of Kula Gulf) from Task Force Commander Admiral Ainsworth. Admiral Ainsworth received one a few days ago from Admiral Halsey. Shifted berth from *Vestal* to *Tappahanook.*

Captain Colin Campbell

Walden L. Ainsworth

Fleet Admiral William F. Halsey

Chapter Thirteen

Historical Postscript to Kula Gulf Battle I

The Japanese destroyer *Amagiri* took four hits in the July 6 Kula Gulf battle. Sufficient repairs were made on her and she returned to the Tokyo Express and found herself west of Kula Gulf on a dark night, August 1, in Blackett Strait.

Shortly after 2 a.m., *Amagiri* spotted a PT boat and rammed it, slicing it in two.

It was the PT 109, commanded by LTJG John F. Kennedy.

* * * * * * * * * * *

The End of the Tokyo Express

The Second Battle of Kula Gulf was as similar to the First Battle of Kula Gulf as any two naval battles ever were. Again it was at night, at close quarters, pitting the "whom" of 6-inch gun batteries against the "swish" of the deadly Long Lance torpedoes. Again, *St. Louis* was hit with one of these torpedoes. This time, the torpedo sheared off the bow but caused no serious casualties.

The coordinated sea and air operations against the Tokyo Express were having a telling effect. The toll of lost Japanese destroyers proved too heavy. So they shifted to barges. Now the PT boats took over from the cruiser-destroyer forces and with coordinated air attacks the Tokyo Express, or "Rat Operations" depending on which side you were on, came to an end about a year after they started. This was a year of the fiercest naval battles the world has ever seen.

* * * * * * * * * *

August 1 Underway for the States at 0800 with *Chenango*, a converted carrier, a tanker Number 73 and three old destroyers. *St. Louis* speed 15 knots. *St. Louis* has the flag personnel and transferees aboard.

August 3 Crossed 180 degree Meridian which makes *St. Louis* observe two Tuesdays.

August 4   Carrier refueled the three destroyers.
August 7   Crossed Equator at 0400 on the 161 degree long.
August 8   Refueled from *Chenango* at 0900. At 1700, headed for Pearl Harbor.
August 10   *Milomi* has engine trouble and is left behind. *St. Louis* and *Hopkins* proceed Northeast at 15 knots.
August 12   Refueled *Hopkins* and gave her supplies.
August 13   Same two ships, course northeast, speed 13.
August 17   Arrived in San Francisco.
August 18   Mare Island Navy Yard. Started on 21 day leave.

A Message From Rear Admiral Ainsworth for the Officers and Men of *St. Louis*

It is a source of great satisfaction to me to be getting the ships of Cruiser Division Nine together again in the combat area, ready to resume activities against the Japs. We have all had a well-earned break, have had leave and liberty at home, have made good our battle damage, and have received new gear and alterations that should make the ship even more efficient than at the time of Kula Gulf and Kolombangara. Due in no small measure to your efforts in those places between January and July, our forces now use Blackett Strait, retire to Kula Gulf for fuel and supplies, and our planes now operate from the airfields at Villa and Munda.

But we cannot rest on past laurels. The job is not done, it is just getting a good start. The Philippines and Tokyo are a long way off, and there are still plenty of Jap ships and planes that must be eliminated. Admiral Halsey has said, "Sink Japs, and more Japs, and keep on sinking Japs." That must be our purpose and our intent. Moreover, the Japs have not yet paid in full for *Helena, Strong, Chevalier, Gwinn, DeHaven*, nor for the bows of *St. Louis* and *Honolulu*. We expect and will still make them pay, many times over.

I extend my congratulations to the newcomers among you. You have had the good fortune to join a ship's company of veterans, all members of a fighting team. To ensure success in battle a fighting team must have an alert, "heads-up" attitude on the part of every

Chapter Thirteen

officer and man, every moment in every day. We must have the jump on the Japs to assume victory.

When we join Admiral Halsey, we shall report "ready for duty." Heads up—LET'S GO.

W. L. Ainsworth

Chapter Fourteen

Captain R. H. Roberts, U.S. Navy, graduated from the Naval Academy in June 1918, a member of the class of 1919, which was graduated at the end of three years incident to World War I. His first duties as a commissioned officer were aboard USS Great Northern (AG9), a high speed transport carrying troops to France. After completion of one month duty, he was transferred to USS Tucker (DD57), a destroyer, and then USS Sigouney (DD81), also a destroyer.

Subsequent to World War I, he served in the gunnery department of the USS Arizona for forty months, followed by fourteen months tour of duty as the navigator of the USS Capella (AK13). This duty terminated his first tour of sea duty, after which he completed a course of post-graduate instruction at the Naval Academy and the Massachusetts Institute of Technology.

Following post-graduate duty, he spent six years in destroyers during which time he served as torpedo and executive officer, commanding officer and squadron gunnery officer; the latter duty was with Admiral Halsey when he was the Squadron Commander of Destroyer Squadron Three.

Following destroyer duty, Captain Roberts spent four years at sea in heavy cruisers, two as gunnery officer of the USS Tuscaloosa (CA37), and two as the staff gunnery officer of commander cruisers.

Two tours of shore duty were spent at the Naval Torpedo Station, Newport, Rhode Island, and his last shore duty was spent partly in the Office of the Assistant Secretary of the Navy; the majority was

Chapter Fourteen

spent in the Bureau of Ordnance, Navy Department. It was from this duty that he came to *St. Louis*, which he took command of on October 12, 1943, at the Navy Yard, Mare Island, California.

**Captain R. H. Roberts
October 12, 1943**

Born in Michigan, and graduating from Allegan High School in Allegan, Michigan in 1923, H.M. Briggs entered the Naval Academy in 1923 and then graduated in 1927. After graduation, he served on the USS Idaho for one year, then on the destroyer USS Farquhar (DD304), USS Zeilin (DD313), and USS Claxton (DD140) for three years. During this period he also spent three months attending the West Coast Torpedo School. In early 1931, he reported to the newly commissioned heavy cruiser *Louisville* for two years duty. In 1938, he was assigned as executive officer of the aviation-minesweeper USS Gahnet and spent eight months surveying Aleutian Island waters in the area of Kiska, Attu, and Adak, which were just taking center-stage in the American media. In the summer of 1934, he reported to post-graduate school in Annapolis, Maryland to take the Ordnance Engineering Post-Graduate course. He completed this course in the summer of 1936, and after a year spent touring Army and Navy ordnance stations and establishments, reported to the heavy cruiser *Tuscaloosa* for duty as the assistant gunnery officer and later as the navigator. Early in 1940, he was ordered in command of the destroyer *Hamilton* (DD141) on duty on the Atlantic Coast making Naval Reserve training courses and operating as coastal patrol.

In early 1940, he was ordered ashore to the Bureau of Ordnance, Washington D.C., serving as the Assistant Director of the Production Division of that bureau, until ordered to duty as the executive officer of *St. Louis* in February of 1944.

Captain Roberts saw his first action from the bridge of the "Lucky Lou" in December 1943, when the ship bombarded the Kieta area of Bougainville.

On St. Valentine's Day in 1944, *St. Louis* was covering American landings on Green Island, north of Bougainville. She lay off the island most of the day without incident, then "six Jap planes, which had been far out on the horizon most of the late afternoon, closed on our port quarter about 7 p.m." Boatswain's Mate I-C Walter M. Brickhaus recounted:

> "They came in to about ten miles, at which point we identified them as 'Vals'. I was pointer on an after A.A. director then, and the trainer was another boatswain's mate by the name of Lee Pierson, from Newport News, Va. Pierson was always talking about his eyes being bad, but that day he tracked those planes out to thirty miles and watched them turn to come back. Only four came in, and these split in two groups, one of the pairs heading right for us.
>
> We opened up everything we could bring to bear, but they were good pilots on a bombing run, none of those screwball kamikazes, and they kept right on coming. One of the planes dropped a stick of three bombs and missed; the other also dropped three. He was lower and two missed, and the other hit us almost amidship. We splashed him anyway. A coxswain named Parnett was trainer on a quad mount, and the bomb bent the outer edge of the trainer's seat he was sitting on and went on through the deck. Parnett wasn't even scratched but he went around for about a week with eyes as big as saucers.
>
> The bomb had exploded two decks below Parnett's seat in a

compartment where some ammunition passers and a relief engineer crew were stationed. One result of the hit was that the after engine room had to be abandoned because of the heat, and as a result, the Admiral received a message from *St. Louis* which is now famous: "Because of battle damage, the *St. Louis* is restricted to speeds above 29 knots!" When it was possible to return to the engine room some time later, all machinery was operating perfectly. Quite a compliment to the efficient engineers.

The blast of the bomb did considerable internal damage to structure and personnel. Electrician's Mate 3/c Bill Murphy was one of the first to enter the blasted area, known as the post-office compartment.

'I was the second fire hose handler to enter the compartment,' Murphy said. 'We could hardly see because of the smoke, but we did see some movement not far from us.' We found four men there, all mangled, but still alive. They died minutes later. Being an electrician, I helped kill live circuits and cut out other circuits. I fought fire and helped evacuate wounded and killed. There weren't many wounded, two or three I think. Most were dead.

Those damn Japs knew we were hurt and they were trying to get us. The destroyers had put out a smoke screen and we were maneuvering round inside it. There must have been about thirty planes in all, and you could always hear their roaring engines. One tin can on our starboard beam would run out the smoke, turn outside fire like hell, and then duck back in. It was the worst night I ever spent, but I guess we have to expect such things once in a while. War sure is hell.

Although considerable structural damage had been sustained, it was considered not beyond the capacity of tenders and the ship's force to effect repairs. These repairs were completed some time in February at Purvis Bay."

St. Valentine's Day at Green Islands
By Larry Fridley

It was on Valentine's Day, February 14th, 1944. I was on watch in the after engine room as a control talker for all the engineering spaces. I had been talking with MM 1/c Rosandich about our last trip into port. He said he had gotten married and was very happy about it.

Moments later, G.Q. sounded and I went to my battle station which was in the passageway next to the Executive Officer's office. I also manned the phones at my battle station and talked last with Kitson F2/c who was in the post-office compartment next door.

I was in the passageway with Lieut. Berton and James P. Jones. Berton was an Arkansas man and well-liked. I had worked in the mail room with him earlier in the war.

Lieut. J.B. Berton was talking about somebody putting a pin through their inner-tube style life jacket and attaching it to themselves. "How stupid can you get?" he said.

Then just a few moments later, Lieut. Berton said for everyone to hit the deck; lie down. I had made it around the corner of the room; just as he got through saying that, I heard the most dreadful explosion I had ever heard. The bomb blew Berton around the corner next to me. All the lights went out, water lines were bursting and steam hissed in the darkness; water was everywhere.

I thought the ship had been split in two and I was still aboard part of her. I realized I still had on the phones and tried to make contact with Kitson, but he had just been wiped out for good. He, of course, was in the post-office compartment that was hit with the bomb. (My battle station for many, many months on a previous trip out to sea.)

Since it was so dark, something had happened that my phones got tangled and I couldn't get anybody anyway. Then someone turned on an emergency battery-powered battle lantern, and there laid Lieut. Berton beside me. He had been struck by a large piece of bowed section of metal, three hooked prongs planted in his face.

What still bothers me is that in trying to get out of the compartment, the guys stepped on the large sheet of metal that stretched all

Chapter Fourteen

the way to Berton's head, and it went even deeper in the flesh.

I was only nineteen years old. I didn't know what to do, but a fast decision had to be made, so with one hand I held the steel plate and with the other I pushed his head back. The metal came out real easy. The blood just gushed out. It got all over me. So with the help of a fireman named Modestinni and Jim Jones we got him topside. A big job was getting him through the hatches, we were still at battle condition.

When I came back from topside I was all wet and bloody, and they thought I had been wounded. I didn't know whether I was or not, except that I felt all there. About a week or so later I found a piece of shrapnel in my chest.

The part I'll never forget was when we assembled later in a group beside the machine shop one deck below, Lieut. Margoles was reassigning us to another temporary battle station and asked for a volunteer to go into the machine shop. Nobody wanted that spot, all that machinery and right on the water line. I should never have been 6'4" tall and standing directly in front of Lieut. Margoles that night, because nobody volunteered and he picked me. I felt I had been given my death warrant. At nineteen, that is the one time I can remember being afraid. I kissed the machinery and I kissed the deck, and also did some praying—which I believe helped—because I felt that was really going to be the end for me.

Today they have a song out which relates very well to my prayer that night. Its name is "Help Me Make It Through the Night." I've thanked the Japs many times for not releasing a torpedo towards us the rest of that night. That was a temporary battle station—thank God.

Later that night or early next morning when I returned to the post-office compartment, I realized a lot of my buddies from the boiler room and engine room were there when the bomb hit—Rosandich MM1/c, who I was talking to when it all started, and others I stood watch with and knew very well such as Carraway CWT, Gustison F2/c, Rosbury F2/c, and Bryant F2/c. I can remember the terrifying heat, flames, and smoke that poured through the ship.

While standing watches in the after engine room, I would leave and then return, only able to stand the heat for fifteen minutes at a time. During one of those watches, I opened the hatch door, and upon closing it, fell flat on my face from exhaustion. I was barely able to get up, but eventually managed to make my way down to my living compartment one deck below—only to find three and a half feet of water at the bottom of the ladder. The chief water-tender, Lucien Gosselin, was at the bottom of the ladder and greeted me with, "The water is a little deep!" "Yes, it's almost to my pockets," I replied. Chief Gosselin said, "It's *in* my pockets!" From then on, he referred to me as "High-Pockets." Chief Gosselin was responsible for the engineering part of that compartment, as there were other divisions on the starboard side. One consolation was that my bunk was a top one, so I was able to climb up on the springs and get a couple of hours sleep. The bedding, however, was in fire and water-proof bags.

The next day, I helped bury twelve of my close friends to the port-side and eleven were buried to starboard. It was a sad affair, seeing with my own eyes some sea animal dragging the canvas sack as it hit the ocean. After that I thought it was a privilege to be buried in a casket on dry land. These were the first war casualties aboard the Lucky Lou.

* * * * * * * * * * *

Marianas- Guam Bombardment

Early in June, *St. Louis* joined one of the large task forces composing the new Pacific Fleet and joined in the softening-up bombardment of Saipan, Tinian, and Guam. Later in July, she was part of the heavy bombardment group which immediately preceded the Guam invasion. At this time, the ship often maneuvered so close to the beach that her machine guns were brought into the action. For such excellent ship-handling, the commanding officer, Captain Roberts, was commended by Commander Cruiser Division Nine; the ship and personnel on the excellence of bombardment performance by Commander Third Amphibious Force.

An unlooked-for result of the Green Island bombing, however, forced the return to the United States. This was the loss of

Chapter Fourteen

one propeller, probably caused by near-miss bomb explosions. In any case, the propeller finally worked itself off during the Marianas campaign.

* * * * * * * * * *

Task Force 58 Off Japan

Upon returning to the western Pacific, the *St. Louis* joined in the invasion of the Philippines and, as we previously related, was severely damaged in the Battle of Leyte Gulf. This damage necessitated her return to the States for repairs at the close of 1944. I—Captain John B. Griggs—relieved Captain Roberts during this period, and when we sailed from California late in January, I was confident in the ability of the ship and her company to meet exigencies of future months. After a trip across the Pacific, which was uneventful and consisted primarily of daily training, we joined the now famous Task Force 58, and were present at the heavy air strikes on the Jap homeland in the middle of March. I must admit that I experienced a most gratifying feeling of pleasure to know that we were returning the Nip's visit to Pearl in 1941 with interest. Of course, even with our superior force, the enemy once in a while broke through our defenses.

* * * * * * * * * *

Enemy Plane within U.S. Formation

"I remember well the one that broke the ice," said Seaman 1/c Raymond E. Greason. "I was on my machine gun station forward at the time. A little after seven o'clock Sunday morning it was, as I recall, we had already dispatched our first wave of planes. I don't remember exactly whether some were already returning or whether it was our covering planes...but anyway, there among our fighters was a Jap "Judy" trying to act as if it belonged there."

"We identified the plane as enemy, but it was in such a position that if we shot at it, we would hit one of our own ships. So with a helpless feeling, we watched it zoom a carrier, let go a bomb, and speed away. It was just a long shot try and the damage to the carrier was negligible. Needless to say, the "Judy" was splashed by our fighters shortly after."

St. Louis is credited with two assists in splashing the Japs during these raids. The raids themselves were preliminary to bigger events, and it was not long before *St. Louis* found herself, with hundreds of other ships of all types, bombarding the coast of Okinawa.

* * * * * * * * * *

Okinawa

On the second day of this campaign, a welcoming package was almost received from the Japs when a midget submarine fired two torpedoes at the ship. One fish passed ahead, and the other just missed the stern. A "straddle" normally means excellent shooting in gunnery, but in submarine torpedo firing is not considered good at all. Luck was still with the "Lucky Lou."

For fifty of the ensuing sixty-one days, *St. Louis* was stationed on the firing line, and eight of the remaining days were spent in replenishment. She was subject to call for the sixty-one nights and fired during thirty-eight of them. That, on the surface, indicated that we had three days and twenty-three nights in which to rest and relax.

But relaxation was not always that easy. A certain organization the Nips had started, called the Kamikaze Corps, made things constantly unpleasant. In the course of those sixty-one days and nights, we had eighty-eight air alerts, fifty-two in daylight and thirty-six in darkness. We are thankful that only eleven of the alerts ended in actual attacks on our unit.

As there are, and must be in every organization, there are many officers and men in every ship who work consistently and well toward the success of endeavors, and because of their stations are seldom in the limelight. I am speaking now of our cooks, radiomen, engineers, telephone repairmen, bakers, phone talkers, etc. These people are always on the job, doing hundreds of little jobs, which are essential to the efficient operation of a large combat ship. They

Chapter Fourteen

seldom see much of the actual engagement, but some of them frequently play a more intimate role than they themselves realize at the time.

For example, take the case of Radioman 2/c Cletus S. Paull. "I'll never forget one morning," Paull recounted recently, "when a shore fire control party sent us an 'urgent', in which it requested us to fire star shells over a sector of shoreline on western Okinawa. We did, and there in the illumination was a group of Jap boats attempting an infiltration movement on the flank. Our marines made short work of those Nips, about 300 or more, and later our spotter on the beach said we had put out the most effective and accurate illuminating fire he had ever seen."

Two messages that tickled the crew as much or more than any received at Okinawa came from two small minesweepers lying outside an East China Sea anchorage, where *St. Louis* had refueled. As the ship was leaving anchorage, a lookout—Emil Sewell of Great Falls, Montana—spotted a Jap "Val" at 15,000 yards bearing down on the smaller craft. The Jap was quickly splashed by our heavy AA battery at about 8,000 yards.

The minesweepers stopped their apprehensive weaving and their signalmen wig-wagged: "We're happy that you happened to be around," and second, "We sure are glad that you're on our side."

* * * * * * * * * *

A Bull's Eye at 8,000 Yard Range

During the eleven actual air attacks, previously mentioned, *St. Louis* shot down, unaided, four Jap aircraft and assisted in the destruction of at least three more. The longest range bulls-eye was scored at 8,000 yards in the incident described above, and the shortest was registered against an Oscar which hit waves less than 200 feet off the starboard bow.

The last-mentioned Oscar was the harbinger of a most unpleasant afternoon. He pounced from the overcast, circled, and roared for our bridge. We, at the time, were guarding a group of minesweepers off Ie Jima, an island west of Okinawa.

The Saga of the Lucky Lou

Seaman 1/c Charles G. Schubert of *St. Louis* remembers this Jap as a "mighty persistent rascal." Schubert said, "We were pouring the lead into him, but he kept on coming until he got close enough to do a little pouring himself. They must be all doped up. He was wild with his first slugs, but in a moment, he was tearing the stuffing out of one of our searchlights. He looked like a sure bet to crash the bridge, but, all at once, he just went limp and plunged into the deep."

St. Louis immediately rendezvoused with other major units, and together they helped repel what had developed into one of the great air attacks of the war.

A carrier task force intercepted and shot down 165 Jap planes, and 115 more were destroyed by ships and air patrols in the Okinawa area. Jap after Jap streaked from over the horizon. Winged specks that drove through almost solid curtains of flak grew upon the vision until they either exploded in the air, splashed in the water, or smashed against the deck or superstructure of an American ship. Records show the Japs lost over 1,000 planes in that one day.

None menaced *St. Louis* directly, or so it seemed, but our guns were flaming until night drew down the curtain on the savage attack. Suicide boats and suicide swimmers were a constant menace to the ship, and required additional patrols and watches. Three times we were taken under fire, by Jap shore batteries, but each time we successfully silenced their guns by counter-fire.

"One of those shells broke up an enthusiastic jam session we were having," recalled Fireman 2/c Henry Merlotti of St. Louis, Missouri, a saxophone player who had worked with bands in and around St. Louis for seventeen years. "Here it was, a fine evening, we were waxing hot and the crew was enjoying it when one of those flange-faces started planting shells alongside us. Of course we moved! We held the session the next night, and except for occasionally being drowned out by the booming of other ship's guns, we all had a great time."

It must be clear by this time that the *St. Louis'* principal function at Okinawa was the supplying of covering gunfire support to American troops. During the sixty-one days that the ship was engaged in this campaign, it is believed that may have set an all-time record for ammunition expended in such an operation by a single

Chapter Fourteen

ship in that number of days.

At the end of May 1945, just prior to the end of the Jap resistance, it was felt that the ship and her crew deserved a much-needed rest, and so we departed from Okinawa and retired to a rear area for rest and relaxation to tidy up a bit.

* * * * * * * * * *

Back North Into Danger

Our ship was ordered back north to Okinawa in late June, assigned patrol to protect shipping in the area. Seemed odd to be there and no air attacks. We were ordered back north as a unit of Task Force 32, around the first of July and our group was assigned the closure of the East China Sea to Japanese forces, plus we were screening for anti-shipping sweeps that were continually being conducted by the outlying destroyers.

* * * * * * * * * *

Mine Sweeping in East China Sea

Our duty was to provide surface and air protection for the ongoing minesweeping operations, and escort for minesweepers with their rigged para-vanes for cutting mines loose in the area. These para-vanes were interesting pieces of Naval equipment. They had the appearance of a large fuel tank which one would have noticed under the wings of an aircraft. Fins and elevators (like the elevator on the tail of an airplane) were capable of being set so these pieces of equipment, when towed by cable from the mother ship, would ride at a pre-determined depth and distance out from the side of the ship, like 100-200 yards or so, maybe more. Not being of this rating, I didn't know this type of information. Each carried a signal flag which protruded out of the water above where it was riding in tow. These para-vanes would be streamed out behind the ship. The ship would, in a drawing, look like the head of a "V" with the arms behind being the cables to which the para-vane was attached.

* * * * * * * * * * *

Cutting Mines Loose

Not being a "mineman," I can only describe what was told to me about these cutting devices. There apparently was a cutter bar—somewhat like the blades of a hedge trimmer—below, which was attached in some manner to them so that in the towing of these devices, if an anchored mine chain contacted the tow cable, it would ride or slide on the cable towards the para-vane because the towing ship was, of course, moving forward. When the chain attaching the mine to its anchor slid along far enough to reach the para-vane, its chain would slide into contact with the cutter bars. The pressure of a foreign cable being pulled into the mouth of these cutters with the para-vanes underway would trigger an explosive charge. This charge would be the closing lever to cause the cutters to slam shut, shearing off the chain from its mine. The mine would then free-surface.

The rigged and running para-vanes would be constantly under observation, when the flag dipped somewhat like a bobber on a fish line. It had made contact. The mine would be sheared loose, and float free. One of the smaller ships would move in and explode it with a 20 mm gun. Firing continually until it exploded. Mines are much larger than you think. They are dangerous and ugly, with horns which contain the detonators sticking out from the sides. They are probably three to four feet in diameter.

* * * * * * * * * * *

Free Floating Mines

"Floating mines are really hairy." All mines in an area as heavily mined as in this set of water were not anchored. Through the movement of the seas, storms, etc., many would break loose and be a menace to all ships; the original navy that had laid the mines was in danger also. They had to be blown out of the water by firing at them.

Destroyers or destroyer escorts (a smaller vessel) were usually the ships that were assigned the jobs of moving in close enough to fire at them with 20 mm's. Loose ones floating were always looked—and found. The lookouts spotted a close one we all remember. It was sighted floating free and practically in our track. It floated past slowly (we were cruising slowly also), down past the side of the ship. They cannot turn quickly at that point, because the wash might cause the mine to move in…and in turn cause an explosion which, if not sinking, would most certainly severely damage and more than likely inflict personnel casualties to a ship.

* * * * * * * * * * *

Mine Watch

As a result of the above near-miss, a mine watch was established during this mine sweeping and clearing operation. "Lucky Me" and a few other deck-hands with…low seniority from our division were listed for this watch. All the deck divisions, to be fair, furnished so many men to stand this lousy watch. One person only…would climb on top of forward turret two, the high turret on the bow, wearing foul weather gear and bundled up; it was uncomfortable there in the wind. We sit on the edge of one of the life rafts secured on top of each turret, given binoculars and told to watch the oncoming sea for floating mines. How I, or anyone else, could have seen one and in turn warn anyone in time for the ship to veer is beyond my imagination. We wore sound-powered headphones connected to a talker on the bridge. It was a certainty in my mind that if we hit one, I was a goner. I surely would be blown sky high off the turret.

* * * * * * * * * * *

Air Strike Because We Were There

One air strike was conducted by carriers of the force against the Chosen-Hangchow area, this was probably to remind the Japanese that a task force large enough to warrant a carrier was in the area, and to keep their heads down or suffer the consequences. The Japanese had very few operating forces in China by this time in the war. We had no fear of land-based planes from China. *St. Louis* retired to in late July, returning to the Okinawa area, anchoring in the Buckner Bay area for replenishment.

* * * * * * * * * *

Operation Over

We were awarded the right to attach another battle star (a small bronze star), for our combat ribbons and this information was entered into our service record.

* * * * * * * * * *

Chapter Fifteen

Back to the Philippines

Finishing our assignment protecting the mine sweeping in the Yellow Sea was another step towards closing the door for Japan. We were ordered south to Subic Bay in the Philippines. This area was a major Naval Harbor and anchorage for merchant, as well as Navy, ships. It is north or Manila on the Island of Luzon.

Making entrance into this anchorage, a ship would travel up a narrow passage about half a mile wide.

We went to general quarters, Condition 2, while traversing this passage. The Japanese troops were known to be on the hills above the passage, and our ship was ever alert and wary to surprise.

A mile or so before opening into this large protected harbor, ships would pass "Grande" Island. This had been an armored fort with huge gun emplacements. These, of course, now were damaged, rusted, and wrecked in general, but a person could see that in the old days no ship could make an entrance without permission. I suppose these dated back to the Spanish American War. A fortification like this with modern aircraft was doomed, but those huge coastal guns would have kept any fleet out in earlier days.

On our way in, we passed two submarines being led out to deep water by a destroyer. The crews, or many of them, were standing topside. We, of course, gave a "port salute," and they saluted as we passed. This was a Naval courtesy and custom to recognize a passing ship, going in or coming out of port.

Those guys didn't look too thrilled to be going out on another "war patrol." Submarines were really dangerous...and the chance of survival wasn't too good. If a crew member made it through five war patrols, they were shipped back to the United States. Many never got the five patrols in. The subs were painted light gray and looked pretty deadly to me.

Destroyers would escort a sub out to deep water, about 3-4 miles off the coast, where they could dive and go about their orders. At least they were safe that long.

Upon entering the harbor, we were directed to an anchorage area. As soon as the sea detail we secured and the anchor dropped, the gangway was put in place, and immediately a small boat carrying office "guard mail" would come alongside with official business mail. Much of this was for the different departments, such as supply advising procedures for re-supply and general ships business.

Working parties were ordered the next day, and I was put on one that would go to a "reefer ship"—a refrigerator ship. There we would get meat, produce, and such. A tank glider (the small boat with a drop front), would pick up the working party, maybe fifteen or so men, and deliver them to the destination. Arrangements were made for what time the small craft would come back and pick us up.

We were directed to a cargo hold, by ship's personnel, according to what our requisition called for. This requisition was, of course, handled and submitted by the ship's storekeeper petty officer in charge of the working party.

Working parties in a replenishment type of anchorage, such as we were in while in Subic, could be for anything. Everything needed to keep a fleet going was available. At any given time we would be getting food; next time, maybe ship supplies. One time I was put on a party that was going to a small store's supply storage; of course, we didn't know that until we got there.

Upon entering this large building and being shown where the requisitioned materials were, our minds started working with ideas. Some of us drifted aside from the main party, and we started dressing. New dungarees, new shirts, and I got a new pair of shoes. What we took off was just shoved behind packing boxes. My old shoes were tore out in the front, and the leather was ruined from salt water immersion so many times. So it was nice to have new shoes.

Chapter Fifteen

On one ship we were getting fruit and such. In the hold where we were working, we found there were crates of honeydew and cantaloupes over to the side of what we were putting in the slings to be hauled up to the main deck. The men were ingenious on this one.

We stacked crates in a manner to make a tunnel over to where the melons were. One at a time, we crawled through the tunnel and then would use our knives and have a melon. The ship's storekeepers watching the stuff from the main deck could not see us, so we got away with it.

On that one, we were down in the refrigerated hold so long that when our working party was relieved to go up on main deck and await our boat back to *St. Louis*, I sat down back of the steam engine running the booms that lifted into and out of the holds. It was so cozy after being in the hold so long. I went to sleep. When I awoke, the working party for *St. Louis* had left. I panicked at once.

I knew we were leaving late that afternoon and this was in the afternoon. Missing your ship in war time was an offense punishable by court martial. I was really in an uproar. I went to the officer of the deck, and explained that I was from the *St. Louis* and had been left behind by the working party. I, of course, told him that I was in the hold working and didn't hear them pass the word.

The signalman got on his lights and relayed a message across the bay by relaying and passing along to other ships, with a target "St. Louis," that they had left one of their working party aboard. About a half hour later, here came the ship's gig sent from the ship just for me. Was I ever relieved.

* * * * * * * * * *

Swimming in Subic

One of the days we were there, we were taken as a recreation thing over to Grande Island, where the big guns were entrenched as I mentioned earlier.

We just browsed around looking at the old rusted guns and equipment and fortifications. Young men can only do that so long. So the first thing someone mentioned was "let's go swimming." There was no beach...but one could carefully wade in the water until it deepened and then swim. We swam nude, and I and several others took off running down the cement pier and just bailed out over the water. While I was in the air, I looked down and saw the outline of a huge Portuguese "Man O' War," a type of jellyfish. I was really struggling, trying to keep from hitting this thing. We had been warned of the painful poison it carried. I managed to just get a few red welts on my side. Good thing I didn't hit into this creature.

I also managed to come up with some tropical fungus infection that appeared and grew in every orifice of my body. The corpsmen painted me all purple for a treatment of some kind. I reactivated this fungus in a warm water pool when I got home; with a dandy earache, I went to an ear doctor. He looked and said, "Looks like home." Dr. Noche was from the Philippines.

* * * * * * * * * *

The August Typhoon

We were ordered to sea about the middle of August to escape an oncoming typhoon. These were terrible storms, like our Hurricanes. The major ships went to sea to ride it out. The small ships could only tie down as well [sic] as possible and hope for the best. Many of the small craft...washed up on the beach, some a good ways.

We met the storm about two days at sea; the ship had attempted to get to the outside edge of the storm to be less severe. As we entered into the storm track, the seas got progressively rougher and the waves higher and higher. At the worst point, we were only turning over about 3 knots of forward progress, and this slow turning of the screws was only...able to control the direction of the ship.

After entering into the storm, the ship started taking huge rolls. The bridge kept the ship pointed into the middle of the troughs with the 3 knots it was turning. At times, we could look up and see green water (solid water) higher than our mainmast, which I have to judge was about 80 to 100 feet from sea surface. The reason I make this guess is that *St. Louis* had 20 foot freeboard....from deck level to water was 20 feet. I am guessing that the top of our mainmast or

Chapter Fifteen

foremast had to be 60 or more feet above feet level.

At times, the solid green water would be way above our heads, and then the ship would be lifted up with water in a huge wave swell… we would be on top and could see across the water for a great distance. Now and then we could spot the top of a mast of some other ship down in a trough.

We witnessed out a mile or so from us, a troop ship, on the edge of the August "typhoon" (oriental hurricane) that had hit a mine. It was in heavy seas and every time it rolled to the starboard side, a hole in its port side would come out of the water and sea water would gush out of it. The hole in the side of the ship was large enough to drive a truck into. We couldn't help at all. The word was that a sea-going tug was on the way to help, whether they made it in time or not, I don't know.

Some of the rolls the ship was taking were so severe that we picked blown wave tops (water) on one side and ran it across the deck off the other when the ship righted itself. Below decks was a mess; locker doors were flying open. In the mess hall, the stacked mess trays and pots and pans were crashing to the deck. On one particularly bad roll, I became so alarmed thinking she wouldn't correct herself that I went topside. When she was fairly level, I tore around to the faceplate of turret four, climbed the ladder to the top and sat down inside one of the life rafts. I was sitting cross-ways with my back against one side and my feet braced on the other. The trouble is that about then, the ship started into another roll, and I was staring almost straight down into the water. I thought, "my god, if I fall from here I will go right in the ocean and no one will even know I'm missing. Plus, they couldn't get me even if they did. On the comeback roll, I again slid down the faceplate ladder, across the deck into the hatch forward of turret four, down the ladder [sic] to the second deck and stayed there.

The storm was most severe and the sky outside was real dark and it rained a lot for about six hours, and then gradually eased up. We went back into Naha Harbor at Okinawa the next day. The damage was terrific to the little ships that couldn't go to sea and ride it out. Some craft was way up on the beach, washed there by the waves.

* * * * * * * * * * *

Pennsylvania Catches One

While *St. Louis* was anchored in Buckner Bay on August 12th, about 300 yards away from USS Pennsylvania (BB38) a Japanese torpedo plane slipped in and torpedoed her, crippling—but not sinking—her. My first thought was that we had taken a hit. Boogies had been spotted on radar, and we were at general quarters in the powder magazine 3 decks below the water line. There was an enormous thud, and the GM 3/c Mike Bazerski [who was] in the handling room, said, "We've taken a hit up forward in the superstructure!" As it turned out, it was *Pennsylvania* taking the hit on her fantail. Sound carries through water so well that [sic] it's frightening to hear the sounds out there.

Burned in my memory is the sound of depth charges rolled over by destroyers. Depth charges made a two-part sound; the first was the firing mechanism going off, and then the main charge exploding. Sounded like a "rap," then a "ker-boom." On the surface, there was just the big explosion, but us powder rats could hear it all. We really didn't like to hear depth charges, there being only one answer: out there stands an enemy submarine. And we were located in torpedo junction.

* * * * * * * * * * *

War is Over

We were thrilled to death when we as a crew were told the Japanese had made contact to set up rules for ending the war. Word was received about August 12th. Late that morning, a white plane with green crosses was met coming out of Japan by an escort of Navy fighter planes. They were really protected. There were planes flying cover above, below, and to the side. I got to see the plane. It landed at Ie Shima, the little island the war correspondent Ernie Pyle was killed on just a month earlier. The opening talks apparently were conducted in the Philippines, and the plane was escorted

Chapter Fifteen

back to the Japanese area of the main island. All planes of the Allied Forces were kept miles away from this area. I assume no sorties were flowing at all that day, nor the following days. The war was winding down.

The night we received word about the war ending, I had hit the sack at 20:00 (8:00 p.m.) to get a little sleep before going on the mid-watch at 11:45 p.m. I was to go on watch that night in the after five-inch gun director. An ensign—can't remember his name now—myself, and two others [were on watch] from 12:00 to 4:00 in the morning. On this watch, we were supposed to be relieved at about 3:45 by the next group of people going on the 4:00 to 6:00 watch.

* * * * * * * * * *

My Watch Station That Night

About 10:00 at night, the lights came on in the compartment, and guys were running up and down the ladders, yelling, "the war is over!" At first I thought it was some prank, but then the loudspeaker came alive and advised the crew to take cover from falling shrapnel from the beach. I realized this must be the real thing. Crew members on the ship were racing around, yelling and waking everyone in their sack to the news.

The Army and Marine troops on the beach in Okinawa went crazy. They were firing every piece of ordnance they could get their hands on in the air. This went on for the longest time, until they ran out of ammunition, I guess. The fleet anchored out, and was taking all the debris from the exploding ordnance.

The five-inch director mount is an enclosed, dedicated piece of fire control equipment that controls two five-inch AA mounts. When in control, it had the ability to absolutely control the tracking and firing. The gun crew in the mount's responsibility was to keep the guns loaded and ready to fire. The targets were selected by the Combat Information Center on radar and relayed to the five-inch director. The director set the ranges, etc., and the guns were fired by electric key from there. Four of us were on watch that night.

Liquor was broken out from wherever it was kept. The

higher-ranking officers were issued some; the crew was out of luck. "But," someone said to the ensign, "can't you get something to drink?" He replied, "I can, but maybe only a small can of sick bay alcohol." This was grain alcohol and perfectly good for drinking if cut down enough with water or juice.

He left the five-inch director and was gone about twenty minutes or so, and came back with a little dark green can of the alcohol. I went over to our turret and got some grapefruit juice powder—kind of like Kool-Aid, only sour. We mixed the two together with water to reduce its strength. During the first drink I took, I thought my insides were on fire. We all had a couple of little drinks; the second drink was better. Then it was gone, but we were out of it anyway. That's all it took. I went to sleep. We didn't get relieved from watch until after 6:00 in the morning, when somebody got it together enough to decide the watch should be relieved. The whole ship went nuts that night.

* * * * * * * * * *

Loafing Was Great While It Lasted

From that point on, we just coasted. The ship's order of the day consisted of holiday routine (no work) each afternoon. We were allowed to sunbathe; the engineering divisions began to get sunburned because they were so white from being below decks all the time.

The loafing didn't last too long. We had a wise skipper and executive officer. Idle hands aren't too healthy. Orders were passed down to the deck divisions to start removing the paint off the wood decks...restoring them to the condition they were in during peace time. The other divisions I can't speak for, knowing only what we did.

The deck hands were issued...paint scrapers, a straight flat piece of iron about 12" long, with one end turned down at a 45 degree angle and a bevel ground on the end. By kneeling on your knees, with your left hand putting pressure on the 45 degree angle, the right hand [would] pull with a dragging motion, and do a good job of

Chapter Fifteen

scraping the paint off the deck. There remained a lot of dents in the wood, because of shell casings...hitting the deck throughout the years. Each dent held a little dark blue-gray paint. Our whole ship was painted this color.

It seems like every time there was free time, out came the paint-chipping hammers and paint scrapers, and all the deck hands were put to it. I, being so low in priority, always got a part of all these jobs.

For instance, some of the older seamen would have much better jobs. One I envied was in charge of the bosun locker; this was a tiny little compartment off the deck on the starboard side just forward of turret four, and under that ladder which one had to take up to 01 level to get past five-inch mount three. We called it "going up and over," because on the other side, past the mount, was a ladder of the same length that dropped down on the after quarterdeck. The chow line formed here, going below to the third deck mess hall.

Anyways, under this after ladder was a bulkhead hatch, which when opened exposed a little area like a clothes closet; in it was kept all the tools and equipment needed to run a deck force: the heaving lines, the scraping tools, various tools like fids and marlin spikes for line work, and a small tool bench with a vise in it. Best of all was our "joe" pot and hot plate. The Navy ran on coffee, I think...What a treat to get a cup of coffee from the division "joe" pot. We always drank it heavy with sugar, and white with canned milk. I don't know if I liked it that way when I came aboard, but that is the way the older hands drank it, and so did I. Monkey see, monkey do.

The entire after deck on the fantail was stripped of paint as best as possible. This took about a week. Then we started to holy stone the deck. This procedure was accomplished by using a primitive tool that was only a firebrick from the boiler room inventory, with a small indentation ground into the middle top. A short piece of swab handle was placed in it, and the kneeling deck hand would put his right or strongest hand down close to the brick on the handle, lay the handle up against the right shoulder for bracing, cross his left arm over the handle, and grasp the right forearm tightly.

A row of deck hands—maybe five or six—would start moving these bricks back and forth on the deck in a strong sanding motion.

Salt water would be run across the deck in a continuous stream; this would keep washing away the grit coming off the brick. This old-fashioned sanding method, which had been used in the Navy since sail ships, ground down the marred and dented deck wood to a smooth surface.

The sun and salt water on the decks quickly turned them back into white decks as they were seen in peace times. We scrubbed the decks twice daily. The wood decks were scrubbed with salt water at 0600 and 1600 every day.

I still can hear in my mind the bosun pipe shrilling over the loudspeaker, and the bosun of the watch announcing, "Sweepers, man your brooms. Clean and sweep down fore and aft. Sweep down all deck and ladders." This was a 0800 and 1600 ritual in the Navy.

The gun divisions were allowed to take off the canvas covers from the muzzles of the guns, which were used for expediency in gun readiness, and replace them with the brass tampions on the barrels. These had been stored since the attack at Pearl Harbor. They were all polished up and looked nice. The war was over for sure.

We, at last, knew we had absolutely made it through and were coming home safe to our family. The experiences at that time of my life consisted of periods of terror, followed by periods of calm, mixed with the pleasures of just being young.

Chapter Fifteen

"Once I Was A Navy Man!"

By Jack R. Jones
For My Shipmates

I loved the sea...I liked standing on the deck during a long voyage, the taste and feel of salty ocean winds whipping in from everywhere—the feel of the giant ship beneath me, its powerful engine driving against the sea. I remember the "quivering" of the ship as she cuts through a heavy sea at high speed...the long rolls when a necessary course prevents heading directly into the swells. The gentle pitch when your ship is happy with the sea.

After a hard day of duty, there is a serenity of the sea at dusk, as white caps dance on the ocean waves...I enjoyed the mysterious night sea. The glowing phosphorescence of your ship's wake in the moonlight...the peacetime lights of the Navy in darkness... bright white masthead lights, the green and red of port and starboard lights...I savored the clear night sky at sea and the uncounted brightness of the stars from horizon to horizon. The nights with low talk sounds mixed in the soft noises of your ship as she slips through the water...The whisper quiet of the mid-watch when the ghosts of all departed sailors stand with you.

I have relished the devil-may-care philosophy of a sea-going sailor, the rising sense of adventure in my heart when my ship puts out to sea. Recalling at time the rough, hard work...but...accompanying it always, the warm companionship of robust Navy talk and humor. I can still in the library of my mind smell the aroma of fresh coffee from dozens of pots in literally every division work "shack," and who could forget the steaming galley urns practically always available to anyone who wanted a fresh cup of "joe"...I liked the clang of working steel, the ringing of a ships bell announcing the hour of the day, the strong laughter of sailors at work, and the sad foghorns.

I liked the ships of the Navy...nervous, daring destroyers... sleek cruisers...majestic battleships...and steady, solid carriers. I like the naming of Navy ships: *Hornet, Enterprise, Sea Wolf, Iwo Jima, Franklin, St. Louis, Indianapolis, Missouri, Arizona,* and many others named for heroes and heroic events of our country.

I like the bounce of Navy music and the tempo of a Navy band... wearing "liberty whites" and "dress blues"...the spice and smell of a tropical foreign port...I like the shipmates I've sailed with...men from the cornfields of Iowa, New York's East Side, an Irishman from Boston, the pleasant drawl of the Texans, and men of the sun from California. They came from all parts of the country, farms of the Midwest, small towns of New England, big cities, mountains, the prairies, all to become men of the sea...**usually sooner, rather than later.**

I like the legends of our Navy and the men who made them...I like the proud names of Navy heroes: John Paul Jones, "Bull" Halsey, Nimitz, Perry, and Farragut...a man can find much in the Navy, comrades-in-arms, pride in his country and people. **A man can often find himself.**

In years to come when thinking of times passed, when the uniform is stowed away for good, a man's thoughts will occasionally return to the sea...he will remember, with fondness, the ocean spray on his face blowing from an angry sea. There will ever come in his memories, a faint aroma of fresh paint from somewhere on the ship, and faintly the echo of hearty laughter of seafaring men who once were close companions. Locked on land, he will grow wistful of his Navy days, when the sea was his life, and a new port of call was always just over the horizon.

Then **SOFTLY** he will exclaim:
"Once I was a Navy man."

In Conclusion

For many, the ships of Pearl Harbor began to dissipate from the circuit of day-to-day conversations, just as the memories of World War II began to fade from the mind and take their place on the pages of history books. For the Navy shipmen that had lived, dreamed, and fought aboard the St. Louis, however, her biography was still very much alive and well. After her faithful service bringing U.S. serviceman home as a part of "Operation Magic Carpet" in 1945, she began her journey through the Panama Canal and into the Atlantic Ocean. Upon arriving at the Philadelphia Navy Yard in June 1946, she was decommissioned.

January of 1951 found St. Louis being sold to Brazil as a part of the Military Assistance Program, where she was refitted. She was named Almirante Tamandare (C-12) and continued her quests on the seas for twenty-five more years. The name Tamandare, selected in memory of Joaquin Marques Lisboa, the Marquis of Tamandare and the father of the Brazilian navy, was one of the most revered and distinguished names the deserving ship could have received. She was the second largest ship in the Brazilian navy, surpassed only by an aircraft carrier which had been purchased from Great Britain.

For her transfer into the Brazilian navy, a familiar face was invited to take part in the ceremonies—Mrs. Robert Brookings Smith, formerly known as Miss Nancy Lee Morrill, the Queen of Love and Beauty who had first christened the USS St. Louis on April 15, 1938. She was presented with a sixty-pound brass steering wheel from the Brazilian navy, an appropriate token given her longstanding relationship with St. Louis. She later transferred care of the steering wheel, in a public ceremony, to the city of St. Louis.

Generations later, the USS St. Louis is still remembered as the first combatant ship to make it out of Pearl Harbor on her own accord on the fateful Sunday, and for her part in overtaking more than 10 percent of the enemy aircraft which were shot down. Such a grand accomplishment is considered just as much a nod to the ferocity of a ship as it is to the bravery and tenacity of the sailors who manned her decks. The men of the USS St. Louis continued to keep in touch through the formation of the USS St. Louis CL-49 Association, founded by Commander (Ret.) Al Seton. The mission of the association was twofold: first, to provide a means for which shipmates could remain connected, and second, to "crank into history the incredible saga of the Lucky Lou," according to Cmdr. Seton. The association held many reunions, the last of which was held in 2008—fittingly, in St. Louis, Missouri.

Another piece of the Lucky Lou's legacy which was maintained was that of the *Hubble Bubble* newsletter. Founded April 13, 1942, it was created during a war patrol in the Pacific to keep the sailors informed of the happenings of the ship and her crew. Al Seton was the founding editor. To this very day, the *Hubble Bubble* is still published and disseminated to subscribing members of the crew of the St. Louis; its articles cover everything historical and current regarding the Lucky Lou. As of 2012, the current editor is Jack R. Jones and the newsletter is in its 41rst volume of publication.

As founding editor, Seton headed up efforts to save the ship by calling and writing, calling and writing—old shipmates, embassies, the White House, the House, the Senate. "Our reading of the Brazilian government is that they were pretty anti-U.S. The Brazilian Navy, however, was in favor of saving it." He got five hundred prints of St. Louis moving through Pearl Harbor amid the smoky wreckage of sister-ships, and sent them to newspapers with his plea for the ship's salvation. "The press pickup was phenomenal," he said, "but you know how newspapers are. Nobody said, 'write to Al Seton!'" Larry Fridley, however, did write him, and that was the first meeting with Al Seton. Larry found out that prior to Seton's Navy time, he only lived about fifteen miles from Marianna, P.A., in a little town by the name of Richeyville. Seton at one time had worked for the Observer

In Conclusion

and Reporter, a local newspaper in Washington, P.A. Larry's wife Louise heard something on the t.v. about the USS St. Louis, and Larry searched for Seton through the post office in July and August 1978—and found him at an address in New York.

In 1977, Tom and Irene Brown established the Lucky Lou Historical Association with the hope of bringing the Lucky Lou back to the United States as a memorial. Their intention was to bring it to Chicago, so that future generations could see and experience the history of World War II and the Pearl Harbor attacks without the expense of traveling to Hawaii. The Lucky Lou Historical Association collected more than seven million signatures in support of their efforts to bring the ship back to the country of her origin. Their motto: "Freedom is not free. It must be earned and preserved by each succeeding generation," embodied their belief that the ship was crucial to the responsibility of each generation to keep the rich history of the United States alive.

In addition to the efforts of the Lucky Lou Historical Association, the St. Louis CL-49 Association assembled a "Temporary Organizing Committee" to begin collaborating on the appropriate legal and political courses of action to save their beloved ship. According to the May 1980 edition of the *Hubble Bubble*, the U.S. State Department phoned the association to inform them that as of April 21, the Brazilian navy had received three offers for the Lucky Lou. The largest of these was a $1.1 million dollar offer from a firm in Taiwan. Although no legislative or Constitutional grounds exist which authorize private citizen groups to utilize government entities—such as the State Department—to funnel messages to foreign governments, the committee still scrambled to once again present requests for a postponement of a scrap sale through the American Embassy, the U.S. State Department, and various other means.

After twenty-five years of service in the Brazilian navy, she was stripped of the guns which had defended her against the onslaught of enemy forces, and in 1976 sat anchored in the Guanabara Bay, waiting for her next set of orders. Four years passed of various outside offers to the Brazilian governments, along with continued attempts by American associations to secure her homecoming as a memorial for her accomplishments in the Pacific. At long last, she was purchased for scrap metal by breakers in Taiwan, despite the best efforts of the organizations who had lobbied long and hard for her return to her birthplace. Since she was no longer functioning, arrangements were made to tow the ship to Taiwan, and she got underway in the summer of 1980. On August 24, 1980, the former USS St. Louis (CL49) sank while under tow to Taiwan. She was just off the coast of South Africa near the Cape of Good Hope.

As fate would have it, the Lucky Lou was one of only two ships from the December 7th attack on Pearl Harbor that was still afloat in 1980. With her sinking, the historical associations who had been backing the ship's return refocused their attention: their new mission was to save the former USS Phoenix, which had similarly been purchased by the Argentinean navy and was being used in the Falklands War as the ARA General Belgrano. Tragically, she also sank, at the hands of a British Royal navy submarine on May 2, 1982. The two ships had fought their way out of one of the deadliest attacks in American history, but will remain at rest in the same manner as the ships they left behind in the Hawaiian harbor that day.

As for Larry Fridley, he continued to stay involved with the St. Louis CL-49 Association long after his days aboard the Lucky Lou were over. He was even wed at the association's 2004 reunion in San Diego- to the newly proclaimed Mrs. Beatrice Fridley. Larry— who had patiently waited for his chance to see Australia during his time aboard the Lucky Lou, before being rerouted to Saipan, Tinian, and Guam—finally got his chance to see the continent when he was knighted at the 26th anniversary dinner of the Hutt River Province Principality by Prince Kevin Gale. He had been a part of the St. Louis crew which had patrolled the nearby South Pacific waters. Five days after the ceremony, he marched in the Anzac Day parade, a day of grateful acknowledgment of the veterans who have fought to help defend the freedom of Australians. He also was an active participant in the efforts to bring *St. Louis* back to the United States. The valiant efforts of Larry Fridley, Al Seton, the St. Louis Association, various members of Congress, and additional supporters are documented in the pages succeeding this chapter.

In Conclusion

Walden L. Ainsworth

Australian Cruiser - Achilles

The Saga of the Lucky Lou

Fleet Admiral William F. Halsey

On December 6, 1981, the forty year anniversary of the attacks on Pearl Harbor, the USS St. Louis Association presented the Naval Academy Museum with an oil painting which depicted the grand exit of the Lucky Lou through the blue Pacific waters of the harbor. Entitled *Coming Out of Hell* and painted by renowned marine artist George Samson, it depicted the USS St. Louis as she steamed through the turbulent, war-fraught waters—quite literally, coming out of hell. In the *Hubble Bubble*'s coverage of the presentation was the reaction of Captain John W. Flight, Superintendent of the U.S. Naval Academy, in regard to the absence of the ship's fearless leader, Captain G.A. Rood: "Well, there have been some beautiful words said here today. There's a real sense of history; I think he is in this room. Not just because of what was already here, but because of what you brought here. I think Captain Rood, or retired Admiral Rood, if he were here right now, would be very proud just like I know your shipmates are very proud at this moment, and we at the Naval Academy, of course, are proud to be receiving this painting. It will occupy and be displayed in a place of honor, I'm sure, for the years to come and perhaps in perpetuity."

In Conclusion

Also present for the unveiling was the extended family of Captain Rood. The *Hubble Bubble* reprinted the words of his daughter, Yvonne Rood Flowers, who stated: "We are all deeply honored and deeply appreciative. And as I was hearing all the inspired—and inspiring—words of the speakers who just preceded me, I thought 'just what would my father like me to say?' I know he would say, 'be brief. Get to the point.' So that I will be, and say simply, we are extremely honored and we will always remember this day with great joy and great pride. And thank you all very much."

The St. Louis CL-49 Association also presented the Marine Corps Historical Center in Washington, D.C. with a brass plate from the ship. The plate, which read "Sgt. of Marines Office," designated the office of the Marine First Sergeant on the ship. It was removed from the ship by the Brazilian navy when they received her, and forwarded to Al Seton. He, in turn, presented it to the historical center during a ceremony honoring World War II seagoing U.S. marines, who accepted into their historical collection.

During her lifetime, the Lucky Lou racked up a winning record which would be the envy of any politician, poker hand, or baseball team. The *Hubble Bubble* outlined these accomplishments in this excerpt: "Lucky Lou went on to become the U.S. Navy's most traveled ship in the first year of the war. In WWII, she earned 11 battle stars and three unit citations in operations from the Solomons to the Aleutians; from Pearl Harbor to Japan. She established a record in naval gunfire with her five 6-inch battery turrets of three guns each and four AA dual purpose 5-inch twin gun mounts. She is officially credited with having sunk two enemy cruisers, five destroyers, one submarine and downing fourteen planes. She has many more 'assists'. Three times, Lucky Lou was severely damaged—by torpedoes, by bombs, and by kamikazes. Three times Domei, the wartime Japanese news agency, reported her sunk. At the end of WWII, the U.S. Navy called her "the ship that couldn't be sunk." The incredible saga of the Lucky Lou is a story of a series of dramatic escapes, each...more miraculous than the previous."

Hollywood has tried to recreate the morning of December 7th and the maritime adventures of World War II's U.S. Navy in grand, technical productions. Songwriters have tried to funnel the energy, the escapades, the homesickness, and the bravery into scores of songs and musical numbers, but the truth will forever be found in the tales of the men who walked the decks of the world's bravest ships. Their accounts, preserved in the plaques, the paintings, the memorials, and the pages of books, clearly depict the heart of fire which powered the United States Armed Forces to win the second of the world wars—and it is their example which set the precedent that our servicemen and women enthusiastically succeed to this day. It is in the memory of their service, and the hope for those to follow in their footsteps, that this book is dedicated.

In Conclusion

Dear Al,

You're doing a fantastic job in trying to save a gallant ship, and I want you to know I'm one to appreciate it. Sure glad I tracked you down. I should be doing police work, but forgot to tell you that I'm in a business that stems from the work I did aboard Lucky Lou.

Besides being in the after boiler room and control talker in the after engine room, I also stood watches in the evaporators. Today I sell the largest line of home water distillers.

Larry Fridley

[check from The Union National Bank of Pittsburgh, Pennsylvania, dated July 22, 1978, Pay to the order of Postmaster, $1.00, signed Larry W. Fridley]

[note from the desk of Larry Fridley, July 22, 1978:]

Dear Sir:

I would like an address search on Al Seton of Staten Island, N.Y. He is a retired Cmdr. Enclosed is my check of $1.00 and I thank you kindly.

Larry W. Fridley

U.S. POSTAL SERVICE ROUTING SLIP	DEPT., OFFICE OR ROOM NO.	
TO: 1 Larry W. Fridley		☐ APPROVAL ☐ SIGNATURE ☐ COMMENT ☐ SEE ME
R.D. #4 2 Washington, Pa. 15301		☐ AS REQUESTED ☐ INFORMATION
3		☐ READ AND RETURN ☐ READ AND FILE
4		☐ NECESSARY ACTION ☐ INVESTIGATE
5		☐ RECOMMENDATION ☐ PREPARE REPLY
FROM: Office of Postmaster Staten Island, N.Y. 10314		EXTENSION
DATE August 3, 1978		ROOM NO.

REMARKS:

Your request for the current address of a Mr. Al Seton is acknowledged.

I regret that we are unable to provide this information without having the last known address since post offices do not maintain directories of names only.

As additional information, a change of address is valid for a period of one year after which such records are removed.

A check in the local telephone directory shows a listing for an "A. L. Seton" (copy enclosed) which may, or may not be the party you are seeking.

Your check for $1.00 is being returned herewith.

J. J. McHUGH
POSTMASTER

ITEM 0-13   (Additional Remarks on Reverse)   ☆USGPO: 1976 — 654-402
Aug. 1976   (Formerly Form 13)

In Conclusion

Fridley Printing Company
20 North Franklin Street
Washington, Penna.
Thursday, January 11, 1979

Dear Al:

I went to the Observer-Reporter today and talked with John Northrop, president and publisher. I became acquainted with him some years ago as a member of the Junior Chamber of Commerce. I expressed our thanks to him and Mr. Crouse for their fine article, Dec. 7, 1978.

Gave him the cover page of Dec. issue of the *Hubble Bubble*, pointing out three important things: 1) Brazil expressed willingness to deal with U.S. officials on return of USS St. Louis. 2) J. Jake Pickle and Congressman Murphy, N.Y., are fighting for the ship's return, and 3) with a little proverbial "ship's luck" we might break some new records. I asked him to do a follow-up, and he was on his way to Mr. Crouse's office as I was leaving. I asked him for permission to print the preview article in the *Hubble Bubble*, and he proudly agreed, especially when I told him about our coverage. Al, I would like a couple copies of the January issue for Northrop and Crouse. I'm anxiously awaiting the January issue, as I am every month!

Will have to close for now, but sure was glad to have met you.

Sincerely,
Larry Fridley

The following telegram was sent on March 28, 1978

TO: THE PRESIDENT OF THE UNITED STATES JIMMY CARTER
c/o THE PRESIDENT OF BRAZIL
BRASILIA, BRAZIL

RESPECTFULLY REQUEST THAT YOU CONVEY TO THE PRESIDENT OF BRAZIL, THE BRAZILIAN NAVY AND THE BRAZILIAN PEOPLE OUR HEARTFELT GRATITUDE AND APPRECIATION FOR THEIR HAVING KEPT THE SHIPWRECKER'S TORCHES THAT ONE PROUD SHIP OF TWO NAVIES- THEIR "ALMIRANTE TAMANDARE" AND OUR FORMER USS ST. LOUIS (CL49) SOLD TO BRAZIL IN 1951 AFTER A WWII RECORD AT LEAST EQUAL TO THAT OF ANY NAVY SHIP IN U.S. HISTORY. IT HAS ALWAYS BEEN OUR HOPE THAT WE COULD ESTABLISH THE TAMANDARE/ST. LOUIS AS A TWO NATION MUSEUM AND HOPE YOU WILL HAVE OCCASION TO DISCUSS THIS WITH THE PRESIDENT OF BRAZIL AND VISIT THE TAMANDARE/ST. LOUIS WHILE IN RIO DE JANEIRO THURSDAY.

VERY RESPECTFULLY, USS ST. LOUS (CL49) ASSN. AL SETON- SPOKESMAN

In Conclusion

March 6, 1978
Mr. Jody Powell
Press Secretary to the President
The White House
Washington, D.C. 20500

Dear Mr. Powell:

"The Big Question- What Will President Carter Do This Month in Brazil???" is the lead story in the enclosed issue of the USS St. Louis *Hubble Bubble* being mailed today.

As editor of the paper, I request a statement from the White House as to whether or not President Carter will:

a. Discuss the future of the USS St. Louis/Tamandare with the President of Brazil?
b. Request the ship not be scrapped so a worldwide campaign to save this historic ship can be launched to bring it back to the United States?
c. Visit the ship while in Rio de Janeiro this month?
d. Make a public announcement as to the fate of the USS St. Louis (CL49).

This is all taken up in the lead story. The rest of the issue is a report on our progress and a background on our campaign, the ship's history, etc.

Sincerely,
Al Seton
Founding Editor USS St. Louis *Hubble Bubble*

The Saga of the Lucky Lou

Tuesday, March 18, 1980

Dear Al,

Thanks for the most wonderful news just received concerning prospective shipowners. I keep reading this over and over, and it just doesn't hardly seem possible, but I pray that it will all be finalized very soon. It's not that I lacked any faith in our association (not for once) but as I think back about all of those experiences aboard Lucky Lou so many years ago, it's hard to fathom what's happening. It's just proof that we're still fighting. I know a few people have worked exceedingly hard to make this possible, and I'm sure others like myself are trying to do what they can, but I'll go one step further: if it requires any kind of crew to bring this precious monster back home, be sure to count me in as #1.

1) I have a commitment to save "Lucky Lou."
2) Get a commitment from city like Chicago for resting place.
3) Let's have a reunion in Chicago as soon as possible.
4) I think we should, as an association, get a group of at least three people and go to Brazil and state our case.
5) As a professional salesman, I would like to be one of these.
6) I believe with the backing of our President, Congress, etc., if I had an appointment with the President of Brazil, I could <u>sell</u> him on the idea to release to us the Lucky Lou.
   a) I would need his background (type of individual he is).
   b) Ship's background while in the Brazilian Navy.
   c) Our trade status with Brazil (they certainly need corn & wheat).
7) I would need the help of an aggressive attorney and possibly someone in politics, such as J.J. Pickles.
8) The approach would be a simple and reasonable one, but if they did not give in to a second choice of a two-country memorial, then it's time to get tough—and I mean tough.
9) What would be the approximate cost to rebuild engineering department capable enough to get ship back under our power, as compared to alternate sources of return?

In Conclusion

10) I think our first big problem is that we have to definitely get tough with Adm. Carter and our Navy Department; they were the ones that erred in the first place, by letting Brazil have that ship.
11) We do have a presidential election coming up in the not-too-distant future, and I think we should use our leverage now. Action for us or else.

Also, please send three extra copies of the *Hubble Bubble* please.

Sincerely,
Larry Fridley

March 24, 1978
VIA EXPRESS MAIL
Mr. Jody Powell
Press Secretary to the President
The White House
Washington, D.C. 20500

Dear Mr. Powell:

Although we have had no response to our press query of March 6, 1978 (copy attached) "What Will President Carter Do This Month in Brazil?" in regard to the former USS St. Louis (CL49), I am forwarding herewith, on behalf of the USS St. Louis (CL49) Association, our first "patch" in seven colors, depicting an actual scene in Pearl Harbor on Dec. 7, 1941. They are being distributed to ship's company and supporters.

We would like the President to have it and if he visits the Lucky Lou in Rio de Janeiro to wear it on a jacket we would provide—a khaki wind breaker available in naval uniform shops. But it wears well on any jacket or blazer.

For your information, I am enclosing also two pages being made up for the next *Hubble Bubble* which will carry stories from all over the country, all of which mention President Carter's visit to Brazil and the fate of the USS St. Louis (CL49).

The attached articles range from "The World's Greatest Newspaper" (*Chicago Tribune*) to "America's Oldest Weekly Newspaper," established in 1788 (*Washington County Post*, Cambridge, N.Y.).

Sincerely,
Al Seton
Founding Editor, USS St. Louis *Hubble Bubble*
And Spokesman for the Association

In Conclusion

Interview with William M. Freeman, *NY Times* writer

Appeared in the *Bennington Banner*,
the *Extra*, and the *Hubble Bubble*.

"I should think a ship like that would have an honored place in America," said Freeman. "I'm extremely surprised that President Carter, an ex-Navy man, didn't say something about the ship last year when he was in Brazil. He was asked by the Association to at least mention the ship in one of his speeches, but he didn't say a word."

Hubble Bubble Excerpt
March 1980

"And even more preposterous would be the thought that the crew of this ship which fought with such distinction from Pearl Harbor to now would be denied through willful inaction by the U.S. Department of State to communicate openly with a friendly foreign nation (Brazil) to forestall, at least, this possible destruction.

While such communication is transmitted by the State Department for some private groups and individuals, it is denied to the USS St. Louis Association, which is acting merely to preserve this nation's heritage, with a nation most receptive to this effort."

In Conclusion

Comments Made by Al Seton at Lucky Lou's Birthday Party
April 17, 1978, in St. Louis, Missouri

"Although the St. Louis Association had not been asked to voice any comment at the wheel transfer ceremony this morning, I couldn't but wonder what I would say during that brief, informal, friendly proceeding if the Mayor asked someone from the crew to speak. The thought occurred on recalling that the Lucky Lou is one of the world's last true gunships. I remember an old saying by gunners that "good gunnery will give you straddles but only God can give you hits." Revising that for this occasion, it could be said that "good gunnery will give you straddles but only God can give you *St. Louis*."

"I received a phone call from the office of the head of the National Security Council answering the two questions we have been trying to get answered. Did President Carter discuss the *St. Louis/Tamandare* with the President of Brazil during his recent visit there? Answer—no. Did President Carter view or visit the *St. Louis/Tamandare* while in Rio de Janeiro? Answer—no."

"The question here today for us then is, 'Should we continue our campaign to save Lucky Lou or should we settle for what we got from Brazil today?'"

The unanimous answer: "Save the Lucky Lou!"

USS. St. Louis (CL49) Association, Inc.

Reason for Being

Every ship association in the United States exists only for the life span of the shipmates or to their ability to hold reunions. Then the association ceases to exist. Until then it's pay-as-you go.

But our ST. LOUIS ASSOCIATION is different than any other ship association. It was formed to be a permanent organization because its objectives were to be permanent. These are:

To crank into history the incredible saga of the Lucky Lou.
To honor and bring recognition to its ship's company individually and collectively.

Reunions for each and every ship association is its life blood and reason for being as long as the shipmates are alive. That was not our sole intent or main reason for being. We organized to meet all laws required with safeguards to protect all our shipmates, the memory of the ship and the honor of the Navy.

There is no necessity for incorporating a ship association as a tax exempt, non-profit group with formal by-laws if it is to hold reunions only for its temporary existence. To hold reunions only, our association is overstaffed and over-regulated.

But we incorporated because we wanted to be permanent, to carry out our objectives through generations. Such incorporation is a must. Most of us feel at present we are woefully inadequate and need widespread, continuing attention from all hands and their families.

The United States for the rest of its history will commemorate December 7 every year with special attention. For that reason alone the ship's incredible performance on that 1941 day will cry for attention. This includes:

1) First ship to go to general quarters.
2) Only ship to get underway and reach the open sea during the attack.

In Conclusion

3) Officially credited to shooting down over 10% of the attacking aircraft that failed to get back to their carriers.

The ship continued its incredible performance throughout the war and had the single honor of having the Japanese surrender all of China aboard the *St. Louis*.

No other ship association was organized by four Admirals. No other ship has an actual battle scene pictured in its logo, the only one in the history of the U.S. Navy. No other WWII ship has more reason to be organized permanently. Keep the faith. Keep a steady strain.

Al Seton
President Emeritus
220 Otis Avenue
Staten Island, New York 10306

The Saga of the Lucky Lou

FAR BACK ROW: Larry Fridley, Ned Peterson
MID BACK ROW: J. Doug Huggins, Charles Probst, Maynard "Sandy" Sanders, Ed Amundson, Jack R. Jones, Al Getchell, Jim Womack, Thomas Harriet, Bill Littlejohn, John Garrett, Dessie Shivar, Robert Darling, John Miller, Harrison Scott, Luke Tribe

FRONT ROW: William "Biff" Harral, Kermit Law, Bob Bucci, Lawrence Beale, Vincenzo Lopresti, Merald Grimm

BACK ROW: Glenn "Blackie" Smyers, Marshall Acton, Guy O'Steen, Sumner Blossom, Elmer Tolin, Art Fischer, Clifton Mannon, Chauncey McCann

FRONT ROW: John Leslie, Bob Fish, Sherman Jones, Severino Federico, Ernest Williams

AWOL: Marty Barnes, Sam Lobaugh, Woodley Lott, Glen Ryel

In Conclusion

Messages Entered In Attendance Log

Most of the shipmates attending the 1st National Reunion in Pheonix, Az. added their remarks in the association's attendance log that was kept in the registration area. Here, in the order they signed the log, are the comments of those making them:

Larry W. Fridley: Glad to be here.
Harry T. Milne: Marines carried the ball.
Albert R. (Al) Pierce: Here's to a good time.
Al Seton: Thank god for Al Pierce, Harry Milne and Jack Welsh.
Whitey Fair: Wanting this get-together for a long time.
James V. Pickard: Great to be here.
Jack Welsh: Great to have you here.
Joseph H. Walters: Hi!
Tony George: Glad to be here.
Manuel "Blackie" De Souza: Be highly pleased to get to see all of you. It's great to be here.
Henry L. Poirier: Hi!
J.T. Womack: April '39 to April '43.
A.B. Minichelli: Welcome to our town sailors.

Eugene Wagner: Plank owner.
Anthony Gallo: Great to be here.
C.L. (Lee) White: Good to see you.
Claude and Ruby Goodloe: Happy meeting.
Bill Rush: Great to be here.
Dale O. Dunham: Come to 41.
John S. Rawls: Good to be here!
George Gilfillan: Good to be here!
John Mazalewski: Good to be home.
Albert W. (Bud) Newhall: Welcome to Phx!
Carl Lucas: Could hardly wait for this.
Rosemary Ralls: Good luck.
Warren J. Swarberg: Hi!
Max A. Cease: Glad I could make it.
Jim Jones and Jean: Fantastic.
Robert E. Drumm: Glad to be here.
WM. R. Breland: Glad to be here.
John Q. Edwards: Finally!
Carl Adams: Here at last.
Ed Barker: She was a good ship.
Julian A. Renfroe: Glad to be here.
Ray and Larnee Peevey: Glad to be here.
Syd Robinson and Leah: My sentiments too.
James R. Merriman: At last.
George Currier: We made it.
Richard H. Lambert and Priscilla: Finally made it. This should be a great reunion.
Martin A. Barnes: About time.
Raymond Moody and Ruth: Good to be back.
W.F. "Biff" Harral: Past time!
Mike Polanski: Good to be back.
Michael Elkovics: Finally made it.
D.O. Martin and Betty: Glad to be here.
Ellie Smith and Mary: Still the same. Glad to see all.
Jay and Lucille MacKenzie: Great to finally have a ship's reunion.
Reagan Hudgins: Great experience.
Nad Peterson: '49'ers forever!

In Conclusion

USS ST. LOUIS (CL-49) OUR HONORED DEAD

In peace, sons bury their fathers.
In war, fathers bury their sons.
  Herodotus, 484-409 BC

TERRITORY of HAWAII - OCTOBER 16, 1941
Hawaiian Operating Area *Aircraft Lost at Sea*

William M. Allee, CRM	USN
W. H. James, ENS AV(N)	USNR

GREEN ISLAND - FEBRUARY 14, 1944
Bismarck Archipelago *Aerial Bomb*

John Boyd Baldwin, MM3c	USNR
John Baynor, CMM (AA)	USN
Berdette Bernard Berton, LT (jg)	USN
James Jefferson Bryant, F2c	USN
Kermit Lee Carraway, CWT (AA)	USN
Harold Stuart Churchill, MoMM2c	USN
Thomas Russell Cline, MM2c	USN
Edwin Warren Flood, MM1c	USN
Earl William Freeman, Y2c	USNR
Richard John Gustison, F2c	USNR
David Herron, MM3c	USNR
Mark Dewey Hill, MM1c	USN
Frank Richard Jennings, MM2c	USNR
Neil Victor Kitson, F2c	USNR
Joe Ben McDonald, F2c	USNR
William Arnold McGuffin, F2c	USNR
Urban Earnest Myer, F1c	USN
Edmund Wallace Null, MM1c	USN
Wesley Francis Olson, MM2c	USN
Joseph Frank Rosandich, MM1c	USN
Charles William Rosbury, F2c	USNR
John Monroe Shuman, F2c	USNR
Donald Stehman, MM3c	USNR

ESPIRITU SANTO ISLAND - MARCH 1, 1944
New Hebrides *Electrical Accident*

Stephen Paul Urbani, CEM	USN

LEYTE GULF - NOVEMBER 27, 1944
Philippine Islands *Kamikaze Attack*

Robert Oren Barrett, S1c	USNR
Robert Henry Bowman, GM3c	USNR
Clyde Roe Boyd, ARM2c	USN
Lawrence Ray Butterworth, GM3c	USNR
Wendell Evans Gordon, S1c, V6	USNR
Vernon Victor Goulson, S2c, V6	USNR
Donald Ivan Griebahn, S2c, V6	USNR
David Florian Janikowski, S2c (GM)	USNR
Robert Neal King, S2c	USNR
Eugene Quay Lassiter, F2c	USNR
Wilson Follis O'Neal, S1c	USNR
Wilmer Ernest Olsen, S2c	USNR
John Marshall Powell, CMM (AA)	USN
George William Shoemaker, S2c	USNR
Sebastian George Vogel Jr., ENS AV(N)	USNR
Herbert Whitaker, S2c	USNR

SHANGHAI, CHINA - SEPTEMBER 29, 1945
Huangpu River *Drowning*

Mervyn Richard Miller, S2c	USNR

They shall grow not old, as we that are left grow old:
Age shall not weary them, nor the years condemn.
At the going down of the sun and in the morning
We will remember them.
  Lawrence Binyon, 1914

LARRY WALTER FRIDLEY

TAMPA, FL 1945

Rate / Rank
WT1

Service Branch
USN

Service Dates
11/1942 - 2/1948

Born
7/26/1924
HAZELGREEN, WV

SIGNIFICANT DUTY STATIONS

- USS ST. LOUIS CL-49
- USS APL-29
- USS ACHERNAR AKA-53
- USS COMET AP-166
- USS ATLANTA CL-104

SIGNIFICANT AWARDS

- ASIATIC PACIFIC CAMPAIGN MEDAL - 5 STARS
- NAVY UNIT COMMENDATION
- WORLD WAR II VICTORY MEDAL

Selected Bibliography

Certificate of Commendation

The Secretary of the Navy takes pleasure in commending the

UNITED STATES SHIP ST. LOUIS

for service as follows:

"For outstanding heroism in action against enemy Japanese forces during the Battles of Kula Gulf and Kolombangara, from July 5 to 13, 1943; the Philippine Islands Campaign, from November 15 to 28, 1944; and the Okinawa Campaign, from March 25 to May 28, 1945. Steaming up the Slot with her Task Force shortly before midnight on July 5 to intercept the Japanese on their nightly run from Bougainville, the U.S.S. ST LOUIS met and engaged a superior enemy force of cruisers and destroyers, sinking or severely damaging a majority of these ships. In another furious night engagement off Kolombangara Island one week later, she assisted in damaging or destroying five more ships of the Japanese cruiser-destroyer force. Constantly harassed by hostile suicide attackers while covering Surigao Strait and the Leyte Gulf landings, she rendered invaluable fire support to our assault forces, and although severly damaged on November 27 during one of the most vicious multiple Kamakaze attacks of the war, continued in action after decisively routing the enemy with heavy losses. As part of the Expeditionary Force during the Okinawa operation, she again provided sustained close-in-bombardment and gunfire support and, despite the constant threat of air-submarine and suicide boat attacks, emerged from this hazardous campaign victorious and unscathed. A resolute and sturdy veteran, complemented by skilled officers and men, the ST. LOUIS rendered distinctive service, sustaining and enhancing the finest traditions of the United States Naval Service."

All personnel attached to and serving on board the U.S.S. ST. LOUIS during one or more of the above-mentioned periods are authorized to wear the NAVY UNIT COMMENDATION Ribbon.

/s/ James Forrestal, *Secretary of the Navy*

May it be known

LARRY W. FRIDLEY

U.S. Navy

served with Outstanding Service and Heroism aboard the

U.S.S. St. Louis (CL49)

from   5 November 1942   *to*   18 August 1944

Selected Bibliography

The first phases of this manuscript began decades ago, when Larry Fridley returned home from his time aboard the Lucky Lou. Over the years, the author has compiled letters, articles from the *Hubble Bubble*, interviews and stories from shipmates both alive and deceased, and excerpts from his personal diaries, firsthand experiences, and records aboard the ship. Due to the number of years over which this information was collected and written, specific information is not available for every single source consulted during research. The author did, however, request verbal or written permission to reprint the details which were provided from each source solicited while fashioning the manuscript. Included below are some of the sources consulted during the expansive construction of this manuscript.

Bobrowitz, Nancy, "Lucky Lou Battle Builds", periodical publisher unknown.

Encyclopedia Britannica Online, s. v. "World War II", http://www.britannica.com/ EBchecked/topic/648813/World-War-II.

Hubble Bubble Newsletter. 1942-2012.

Naval History Heritage and Command, "Online Library of Selected Images: U.S. Navy Ships. USS Saint Louis (CL-49), 1939-1951", http://www.history.navy.mil/photos /sh-usn/usnsh-s/cl49.htm.

—"USS St. Louis, Reports of Pearl Harbor Attack." http://www.history.navy.mil/docs/ wwii/pearl/ph84.htm.

USS St. Louis (CL-49) Association, Reunion Program, 1987, 2000, 2004, 2008. Reprinted with permission.
—, "Hubble Bubble Birth", http://www.ussstlouis.com/ Hubble-Bubble% 20%20born.htm.
—, "Official History", http://www.ussstlouis.com/official_history.htm.
—, "War Diary", http://www.ussstlouis.com/war_diary_1941-46.htm.
—, "War Diary 1941-46", http://www.ussstlouis.com/war_diary_1941-46.htm.

World Naval Ships, "Histories of Ships of the Brazilian Navy", http://www.worldnavalships.com/brazilian_navy.htm.

CPSIA information can be obtained at www.ICGtesting.com
Printed in the USA
BVOW020931210113

311030BV00005B/15/P